A WALLOWA GAL

Columns written by Katherine Stickroth
and published in the
La Grande Observer and *Wallowa County Chieftain*
newspapers

2015- 2019

Katherine Stickroth

Copyright © 2020 Katherine Stickroth

Publisher
Katherine Stickroth
whcommunications7@gmail.com
awallowagal.com

Printer
Ingram Spark
www.ingramspark.com

Book and Cover designs
by Linda Bauck, Wallowa, Oregon

ISBN Number 978-1-0879-2690-2
Library of Congress Cataloging-in-Publication
Stickroth, Katherine

1. Woman's self-discovery--humor--adventure
2. Travel
3. Women's life
4. Personal growth
5. Wallowa County, Oregon--Wallowa Mountains--Wallowa Lake
6. Rural community--farm and ranch life--military veteran family
7. Nonfiction--memoir

Front cover photograph courtesy Ellen Morris Bishop, Enterprise, Oregon.
Back cover photograph courtesy of Whitney Chandler, Joseph, Oregon.

Dedicated to Janie Tippett

and all the other beautiful, hard-working, thoughtful, resilient, adventurous, tender, strong, loving, intrepid, smart, powerful, and accomplishing women of Wallowa County.

You inspire me.

ACKNOWLEDGEMENTS

Thank you to Eastern Oregon Media for permission to reprint these columns.

Gratitude is extended to editors Andrew Cutler, Rob Ruth, and Paul Wahl for the opportunity to write this column for their newspapers.

The photographic talent of Ellen Morris Bishop cannot be denied. I was quick to notice her eye for light, and asked if she would photograph Petey and me for the book cover. I was not disappointed in the image she captured. As editor of the Wallowa County Chieftain she gave me the opportunity to write for her newspaper as a freelancer after I recovered from my brain injury. Thank you, Ellen, for helping me get back on my feet again as a writer. You are a kindred heart in our love for Wallowa County and for our dogs.

Linda Bauck, this book would not have happened were it not for your book design skills and encouragement. Your insistence on adding photographs was the perfect idea. I'm laughing right now remembering our giggles over these stories. I brought this project to you based on your other lovely publications and now have gained a friend. From the bottom of my heart, thank you!

Photo credits:
All photos are courtesy of the author except:
- Linda Bauck: 4,18, 43, 47, 48 (single quail). 57, 67, 75, and 77.
- Ellen Morris Bishop: front cover photo.
- Janie Tippett: p.8 from Janie's book *4 Lines A Day* and p. 23.
- Frances Buckles: Open Range, p. 119.
- Joe Cunningham: 114.
- unsplash.com: Casey DeViese: 25, Robert Bye: 26, Mila Young: 68, Megumi Nachev, 73, Simon Hajducki, 94, Jim Strasma, 96, and Aleksi Tappura, 112.
- Freeimages.com: 7 and 89.

I especially thank and praise God for leading me to Wallowa County. It was a good idea.

Introduction

Wallowa County (wuh-LOW-uh, rhymes with cow), where businesses support the farming and ranching families and the agricultural community supports us all.

Wallowa County, where wildlife creatures outnumber the residents and are known like neighbors. Deer, seeking refuge from wolves and mountain lions, patrol the streets. They are admired for their beauty, and at the same time, leave frustrated gardeners.

Wallowa County, where history is compiled of family narratives that ensure the esteem of community, yet monuments stand marking the Nez Perce decampment, Chinese massacre and black loggers of Maxville.

"When did you land in Wallowa County?" is often asked a newcomer. I visited in 2007 and landed in October 2013 to explore not only the breathtaking landscape but to determine what a 56 year old, empty-nester mother and grandmother, widowed and therefore single woman is to do with her life. I felt lost, both within and without. With two sons happily married and raising their children, they had no time for me, and I refused to be "Mom on a shelf," waiting for the rare times they might call.

My husband died in 2009, my best friend and soul mate. Navigating a life without him and burdened with unexamined grief, I was floundering. Making my own decisions without his wise counsel had consumed my time with cleaning up mistakes of my own making, rather than living.

I landed in Wallowa County and soon wondered if I was on another planet. The culture was different from the Deep South where I was raised. Only a few miles of paved roads. No traffic lights compared to the 17 I endured to go shopping at the mall. People here are friendly, yet not wanting to get involved with newcomers who rarely stay for long, juxtaposed to Southern inclusion where strangers are treated as family.

Wild places.

"Don't get into anything you can't get out of," I was advised by an old-timer.

From 2015 to 2019, I shared wanderings, discoveries and impressions of my experiences through my column "Wallowa Gal." It was rare to get any feedback from the readers. Yet one sent me an email encouraging me to continue.

Another said, "I cut out your column and gave it to a veteran friend of mine. It was exactly what I've wanted to say to him..."

And yet another advised, "I'll tell you when you're on the wrong track." Such reticence had me laughing all the way home.

Publishing this collection of lighthearted, rarely serious stories is a gift of gratitude to my Wallowa County family, my readers. Thank you for tolerating my silly questions and seemingly inappropriate behavior. Adjusting from the South Mississippi culture to Wallowa County life was messy at times.

I am deeply grateful for the writing group known as "Write Women": Janie Tippett, Ruth Wineteer, Evelyn Swart, Pam Royes, Leita Barlow, Annette Byrd, Maxine Stone, Pat Adelhardt, Idella Allen, and Cathy Putnam – women with strong voices who helped me find my own.

Readers, thank you for sharing your "quiet places" where the locals go when tourist season peaks. I visited them often as I adjusted to my new life.

And thank you for sharing your personal stories, prompted from my columns. That you would open your hearts to an "alien" who seemed to come from who-knows-where... well, your stories are safe with me.

Katherine Stickroth

TABLE OF CONTENTS

A WALLOWA GAL

The title of this column is derived "tongue-in-cheek," in that I have lived in Wallowa County for only twenty months and have no claim to ancestry or longevity that would qualify me as a true Wallowa gal.

My friend Janie Tippett laid this moniker upon me. After pulling up to her house for a visit last summer, she came out and cheerily greeted me as I stepped out of my truck, "You're a Wallowa gal!"

Puzzled, I asked, "What do you mean?"

She pointed to my rear fender above the wheel. "See that manure splashed on your truck? Every Wallowa gal has that. You must have driven through cow pies while coming up the drive."

I burst out laughing. This city girl from the South had different ideas about how to recognize whether I belonged to a place. But apparently, in Wallowa County, once one is baptized with the excretions of a bovine creature, she is "in."

"This is different!" I thought. I've said that countless times since I landed here.

Each morning I open the shades and am greeted by Chief Joseph Mountain rising outside my bedroom window. I pull open the living room curtains and Ruby Peak says, "Good morning!" Countless times my first words of the day are, "I can't believe I get to live here!"

I walk to my neighbors' house down the street, where we discuss that day's plans. They are included in my gathering of elder friends I could collectively call Wallowa Dad and Wallowa Mom. The wisdom they have shared with me has laid the foundation for my quick assimilation into Wallowa Life. Their lessons have included how to drive safely on snow and ice, how to plant a garden, and the intricacies of fence repair, including building rock jacks.

When I walk the sidewalks of Enterprise or Joseph, I am greeted by new friends I now count as family. I meet newcomers with the most unusual stories of how they "landed" here.

January 2016 will mark two years since I began calling Wallowa County my home, and I wouldn't trade anything for my experiences in meeting a new landscape, a new culture and especially new people who think so differently from what I'm accustomed to. In this column, I will be sharing my encounters from these past months and the days to come with a sense of delight and wonder, seasoned with humor and a slight Southern accent.

Hope you come along for the ride.

WHY THE WALLOWAS?

The Lower Valley as you come out of the Wallowa River Canyon as seen from an overlook on Smith Mountain.

My husband had been from Coos Bay and throughout our marriage he had begged that we move to Oregon. I thought all of Oregon was like Coos Bay, its major downfall being next to the sea. Having survived many hurricanes while living in Mississippi, the most devastating being hurricanes Camille and Katrina, I wanted no part of ocean life and respectfully declined that idea.

In 2007 Richard suggested we go on vacation to anywhere in Oregon. I agreed, as long as I could plan the trip. A web search led me to Joseph, Oregon and I fell in love with the scenes which reminded me so much of Lewistown, Montana. There, Richard and I had met, married and lived for six years. When we later moved to Mississippi, not a day passed that I didn't long for those mountains and plains.

After driving across the country, we entered the valley where my eyes fell upon the Wallowas. I immediately knew I was home.

That week spent touring the area, including Baker City, proved I could indeed live in Oregon. The Oregon Trail Interpretive Center was the final persuasion. Richard was a professional storyteller who recounted stories he had gleaned from the diaries of pioneer women on that long trek.

We headed home, inspired by his dream to be involved with that history organization. I would get mountains.

Within five months I gladly announced the last bill had been paid which freed us to move. But he said, "I don't know why, but my gut is saying now is not the time."

The next month he was diagnosed with terminal cancer. Twelve months later he was gone. Through all of that, and the dark months which followed, the Wallowa Mountains always loomed in the fog of my mind, as though calling "Come."

I began to see daylight four years later. My sons, Matthew and Sam, suggested I move close to them. I now wonder if they sensed my restlessness and wanted to keep an eye on me. Upon visiting them to consider such a move, two things became apparent:

1. They wanted to boss me around.

2. I could not control my urge to advise them on how to raise their children. They felt very comfortable declining my wisdom, thank you very much.

With this useful information, I loaded my Trailblazer and headed west.

La Grande Observer, "Wallowa Life Page," September 9, 2015.

LET'S SEE

Wondering if I could make it on my own, I directed my travel to Wallowa County, where my last good memories with Richard resided. Maybe I could determine what to do with my life with that connection in mind.

I arrived in Enterprise, Oregon, the night of October 30, 2013. Exhausted from the 2400 mile journey, I checked into the Ponderosa Motel, which I was pleased to discover was pet-friendly. My four-legged family members were with me: my little Aussie named Brownie, and Mosie, a calico cat.

Though I lived in the South for most of my life, my years in central Montana had taught me certain unspoken rules to adjust quickly as a newcomer to a small western community, the first being:

The best way to find out the character of a town is have breakfast at the local café.

So early the next morning I walked to Best Friends Restaurant on the other side of the courthouse. The "Junk Omelet" emblazoned on the window invited me to a good meal. I pretended to be interested in the art hanging on the walls as I waited for my order, but the truth is, I was listening.

Other patrons were excitedly showing the screens on their cell phones to each other, asking "Have you seen it?" When the door jingled and a familiar person entered, he was greeted by five phones raised in the air pointed toward him, "Have you seen it?" cried in unison. It took a few minutes, but I finally figured it out.

A moose had come to town.

I forced myself to stare at my breakfast and didn't need to salt my omelet. My tears did the job, from quietly laughing in delight until my stomach folded in half.

I thought to myself, "Let's see. Where I come from, most of the conversations are about unhappiness with the government, the Mideast conflict, the economy, poor health and Social Security. Here, today's topic is a moose came to town."

My heart smiled with delight, "I think I want to live here."

In the days to follow, I spent time soaking in the landscape and questioning whether I could actually pull off a move halfway across the country. I would have to dig deep to find the courage to do this alone, and I had never thought of myself as a brave woman.

I sat at the foot of Wallowa Lake and remembered years ago Richard with his camera, searching for a spot to take the perfect photograph of that sublime scenery. What would he think?

"Absolutely!" my mind echoed with his deep voice and the image of his smiling face.

La Grande Observer, "Wallowa Life Page," September 23, 2015.

Years earlier, Richard had convinced me others would enjoy my writing, which I only considered a hobby. I then had a few things published in Montana. But I parked my writing when we moved to the Deep South.

Pondering my future in Wallowa County, I wondered if I could write again. Thus the decision: I would not introduce myself as an engineer, which had been my career, but as a writer, just to see where that would take me.

I asked a docent at the Josephy Center in Joseph about available housing in the area. She gave me the address of a writer friend who was about to move from a rental. This led me to Ruth Wineteer and though the house had already been rented, we had a delightful conversation about the writing life.

Mary Marks

The weekend approached and loneliness crept in. I awoke Sunday morning thinking, "I've GOT to meet some good people." Ruth had mentioned she attended Joseph United Methodist Church. Although I didn't identify myself with that organization, I drove there hoping I could sit with her.

I have a long history in the Bible Belt of the South, where it appears sedate church people attend strict religious services with somber countenances. The culture is such that once a local asks a newcomer, "What's your name?" the next question is, "Where do you go to church?"

Seated by Ruth, I observed the microphone being passed around for attendees to ask for prayer or to praise answered prayer. A lady with a long white ponytail on the front row spoke.

"I have a rooster named Fred who is causing trouble in the hen house. I don't feel like plucking him, but he is good for eating. So if anyone wants a rooster to stick in the pot, they can come get him. I just don't have time to pluck him."

The rooster announcement caught me off guard, and I fought the giggles. Ruth afterwards introduced me to Fred's owner, Janie Tippett.

I had never met a real author and I purchased Janie's book, Four Lines A Day, where the life of Imnaha's Mary Marks is recounted. I was enthralled with how this western woman lived, especially how she packed into the wilderness to cook for her husband's cow camp. The full impact of Mary's resilience, courage and resourcefulness became apparent when I wound through the canyons on the highway to Imnaha.

Renting a U-Haul was definitely how my belongings would be transported to Wallowa County. Until I read 4 Lines A Day, I doubted my ability to drive a loaded truck alone across the country.

But after turning the last page, I thought, "If Mary could do what she did, I can do this, too."

La Grande Observer, "Wallowa Life Page," October 7, 2015.

THE MOVE

Having kenneled my pets Brownie and Mosie in Joseph, I flew from Portland to my hometown, and sorted through my belongings. Every five minutes I asked myself, "Why do I have so much STUFF?"

I warily monitored the weather between me and northeast Oregon, for I had been warned, "Once winter rolls in, you may not make it back until spring."

A winter storm descended on the West of such magnitude the initial use of "Polar Vortex" was established by The Weather Channel. I grew anxious with each passing day of watching TV, where semi-trailer trucks slid off highways. An extended separation from Brownie was worrisome, for we had never been apart this long.

On week four, a ten day period of clear skies was forecasted as the polar vortex moved east. I hastily reserved the rental truck.

My helpers were my niece and two self-employed brothers who called their business "Stress-Free Moving." Perhaps enamored with an old lady on an adventure, their questions and jokes indicated they had formed my own personal fan club.

If someone complains, "Young people don't know how to work anymore," I challenge that. Unsupervised, these three kids did a great job in packing and loading the truck.

Soon after leaving my home, with a portrait of Sacagawea emblazoned on the side of the truck, I nestled within a convoy of large semis. It was fun to be sitting so high behind such a powerful engine. At a stopover I texted my fan club, "I found my Inner Truck Driver" and cracked up at their responses.

After filling up at an unmanned gas station at Potter, Nebraska, I discovered my keys were locked in the vehicle.

I had just passed through a terrible dirt storm (not dust storm) with poor visibility and was already rattled. Tumbleweeds floated past as the wind whistled overhead. There was no one or any vehicles in sight. I gathered my thoughts and started walking toward a seemingly deserted town.

I came upon a tavern where a handful of ranchers were eating lunch. It took a few hours, but soon I was back on the road.

Make no mistake. Regardless of what you see on television, there are still good people in our country.

La Grande Observer, "Wallowa Life Page," October 21, 2015.

A large part of this new adventure was about me making my own choices for the first time of my life and proving I could do this successfully.

Before going south to get my things, I chose a manufactured home with two feet of snow blanketing the large lot.

"I'll have a lot to mow in the summer, but I'll deal with that then," I thought.

Enclosing all of this property was an impenetrable metal fence and a tall lockable gate, providing much needed security. Though others commented how brave I was to make this change, deep inside I was terrified.

Arriving after a seven day journey in the rental truck, I pulled up to the new abode which now had no snow. Instead, a large graveled lot with a small patch of grass around the house lay before me. I met my neighbor soon after unpacking and inquired about the gravel.

"It used to be a salvage yard, with abandoned cars and trucks," he said.

I laughed at myself. My first big decision, and I had landed in a junkyard.

I mused, "I hope my boys never find out."

As the days passed, I realized for the first time in my life, I was alone. With no obligations, I was completely responsible for my life and the direction it would take. Pen and paper in hand, I reflected on my past- for 56 years, what worked and what didn't. Taking breaks, I began to meet friendly people and would join them for coffee or excursions into this beautiful wild land.

They were amused at my parting comment, "Well, got to get back to The Compound." This place had become like a self-imposed retreat, to quiet myself for a time of soul-searching.

I found beauty in that former scrapheap. Upon a full moon night, the broken glass from countless shattered windshields shimmered as a field of diamonds. During the day, I wandered about, picking up various shards of colorful plastic and chrome. A killdeer couple nested three clutches of babies. A family of quail gathered on my porch to eat the bird seed tumbled from the feeder overhead.

One day, I awoke to the property owner dismantling the gate. He had said from the beginning he planned to do so, but I still panicked. Then an image came to mind, as though God was saying, "Okay, little birdie. It's time to leave the nest!"

Friends helped me find a home with a breathtaking view of the mountains. Settled in now, and with a new confidence, this Wallowa Gal couldn't be happier.

La Grande Observer, "Wallowa Life Page," November 4, 2015.

My husband Richard was a Vietnam veteran and retired with 25 years of military service. He was deployed twice to that Asian battlefield. Laughing, he'd say, "When I saw they were going to send me a third time, I left the Army and joined the Navy. They sent me back over anyway, on the Tolovana."

Those were rare times when he found humor about anything in his Vietnam experience. He held those stories close, but occasionally he revealed different horrific experiences that to me were beyond comprehension. At first I reacted with more questions or tears, and he would close up again. He didn't want his stories to hurt me.

So I learned to be silent and simply listen with a poker face. Upon finishing, we'd sit quietly. Then I'd reach and hold his hand, saying, "I'm so glad you made it home alive and that you are with me."

In just a few moments he would step outside and sit on the porch, smoking a cigarette with our dog Brownie at his side. As I watched Richard through the window, I wanted to go put my arms around him and just hold him.

But something inside said to leave him alone, give him his time and space.

All I knew to do was honor the unseen sacred places of his heart by creating a home of peace, of safety for his mind and emotions, with little stress to trigger him. He never asked for anything, so it was a challenge to meet his needs.

He was diagnosed with a cancer defined as a presumptive disease from Agent Orange exposure. I can only describe that year as a living hell of keeping him alive, battling the V. A., the medical system, and the side effects of chemo.

A few days before he slipped into unconsciousness, he called me to his side.

"You don't talk much anymore," he whispered.

"Anytime I begin to open my mouth, I choke up, and I don't want to upset you."

He reached out his arm for me to lay next to him, and I wept in the quietness of our friendship.

"I only have one question for you," I finally sighed.

"What's that?"

"Do you know you were loved?"

He chuckled, "Oh, yes!"

My veteran is buried at Willamette National Cemetery. He has an awesome view of Mt. Hood. Not a day goes by that I don't think of him, what he meant to me and what he did for our country.

God, how he loved America.

So on this Veterans Day 2015, I thank all our veterans with a salute, then a warm hug.

I'm so glad you made it home.

La Grande Observer, "Wallowa Life Page," November 11, 2015.

A friend invited me to her church service and then to the luncheon to follow. I am familiar with the congregants there, yet a man about my age I'd not seen before caught my attention. His dress, hairstyle and deportment were not usually seen in Wallowa County.

With our plates full from a run through the buffet, my friend sat to the right of me; the minister sat across from me, and the object of my curiosity sat next to her, across from my friend.

I observed the following conversation:

FRIEND (who never meets a stranger): "Where are you from?"

MAN: "Hollywood, California."

"What do you do?"

"I work in the film industry."

"I'm from Lincoln, California."

The man seemed more interested in the food than my friend's inquiries.

Seeing chit-chat wasn't getting her anywhere, she nearly boasted by saying, "My 13 year old granddaughter got a buck deer yesterday. It was her first."

His face lit up with a smile as he lay down his fork.

With genuine interest he replied, "I'm so glad this is the first time she got her butt in gear."

The ease with which he said this made it appear that discussions of whether someone's butt was in gear or not was a common topic in Hollywood.

I nearly choked on my food to refrain from laughing. I looked at my friend for her reaction, then looked at him. He smiled at me to share my friend's good news. I looked at her again.

My friend didn't "get" that he had misunderstood.

I slowly enunciated, with a firm yet friendly tone, "She said HER-GRANDDAUGHTER-GOT-A-BUCK-DEER, not SHE-GOT-HER-BUTT-IN-GEAR."

Perhaps it was the background noise of chatter in the small basement which kept him from hearing me correctly, for he only nodded in appreciation that I repeated her good news. I wanted to climb over the table, hold his face so I would have his sole attention, and clarify that "IN-WAL-LOWA-COUNTY-WE-DON'T-CONVERSE-ABOUT-BUTTS-IN-GEAR, WE-TALK-ABOUT-HUNTING-AND-BUCK-DEER!"

But I was a guest, after all, and restrained myself to not embarrass my friend. "Let it go, Katherine," I repeated in my mind. "Just let it go."

This episode became a gift to me. On restless nights when I am trying to go to sleep, this comes to mind, and I have to bury my face in a pillow to prevent my neighbors from awakening in the dead of night to hysterical laughter.

La Grande Observer, "Wallowa Life Page," December 2, 2015.

In keeping with the Bible's saying, "A merry heart does good, like a medicine...," the local hospital has acquired something which incorporates humor to enable a speedy recovery for its patients.

As a hospitalized friend rested nearby, I sat in one of the tan leather recliners accenting the room.

Not finding a lever on either side, I spied its cord plugged into the wall. The remote was found in the depths of the cushion. I pressed what I thought was the appropriate button.

The back reclined to nearly horizontal, though my feet stayed on the floor. Stretched out like a deer ready to be gutted, I felt for another button because I couldn't raise myself to get a sure look at the remote. Up I went, back to square one.

I reviewed the buttons again, certain I could figure this out - I was an engineer, after all. But in the pressing of the next button, I left that career and became a bronc buster.

My feet flew up with my knees nearly knocking my teeth out. Off balance, I threw up my right hand in proper style and inadvertently pressed another button which almost launched me into a somersault over the back of the chair.

My natural inclination was to exit the beast, but it refused to turn me loose. The rodeo continued as I frantically mashed every button.

My friend, who had been sleeping, awakened to the buzzing of the chair's motor off and on, coupled with unbridled curses that flew from my direction. I don't normally talk that way, being a writer who cherishes words. But for this moment that colorful language was the extent of my vocabulary.

"What are you DOING?" she queried.

I didn't have time to talk, because the ride was on. She observed for a few minutes then broke into the giggles. I started laughing too, initially making things worse. Whenever I laugh too hard, my eyes squint shut.

The blindness turned into a blessing, however. I dropped the remote, and the buckskin bronc finally settled down. My feet were raised in thanksgiving and praise, with my head nearly touching the floor.

Fashioning some kind of roll where I piled onto the floor, I felt like kissing the ground.

"I think I went past 8 seconds," I gasped.

By then we were in such hysterics, I had to remind my friend she was sick and to act accordingly. Very soon she was released from the hospital.

I was glad to be a part of my friend's cure, but now when visiting patients, I stand by the bed and warily eye the bronc's invitation for another ride.

La Grande Observer, "Wallowa Life Page," December 16, 2015.

Before leaving on a weeklong trip to visit my boys last December, friends Manford and Vera Isley asked if I wanted to put up a Christmas tree before I left. I decided not to bother with it, though it would be my first Wallowa County Christmas.

That week, my grandmother-heart enjoyed a wonderful dose of 5 grandchildren under six years old. I taught Colston and Silas, the two older ones, how to bake Christmas cookies. The next two, Annabella and Tate, gave me sideway glances, trying to determine who I was.

And baby Stanton crawled around in the melee, often getting stepped on.

Soon, however, all children clamored for my lap when I announced it was time for their book reading. I couldn't have been happier.

By phone the Isley's kept me apprised of pets Brownie and Mosie who were left at my house. These were constant reminders of my life in Oregon.

I was exhausted as I debarked my return flight. I knew sleep would be beneficial, but was so stimulated I decided to head home. I drove along the Columbia River near midnight and fatigue fueled debating thoughts of whether to move back to be close to the children, or follow through on my new life.

Pendleton. Tollgate. Inching over the Minam, the quibbling continued in my head.

"Should I go back?"

"No. This is your life now."

"But I miss my grandkids."

"Think of your beloved mountains, your friends, and your writing."

"It's too dark to see the mountains right now."

"Believe me, they are still there."

"But where do I belong?"

In early morning blackness, I passed through Wallowa, Lostine and Enterprise sleeping in their illuminated holiday decorations.

Joseph looked like a Christmas card.

"No one even knows I'm back," gasped my last tired thought.

I made a few turns and approached my neighbor's side of the tall board fence between us. My house appeared, with the front curtains pulled open.

Through my picture window stood a Christmas tree shimmering with bright colorful lights. It seemed to shout with glee, "THIS is where you belong."

On that silent night, I rested my head on the steering wheel and cried, so grateful for Manford and Vera.

Within minutes my Brownie dog was wiggling in my arms, and Mosie was at her dish, insisting on food. Yes, this was my home, not because of the unseen mountains looming in the darkness, and not because of my writing, but because of the meaningful friendships I've gained here, people I claim as my "family by heart."

Merry Christmas, everyone, and enjoy your family, whomever they may be.

La Grande Observer, "Wallowa Life Page," December 23, 2015.

In conversations with friends about spiritual matters, I have often said, "Well, God isn't Santa Claus." After last week's Christmas, however, I'm not so sure.

In June 2015, I had to have my dog Brownie put down. It's still hard to talk about that heart wrenching time. She was a rescue dog, Aussie/Terrier mix. We had weathered some tough times over 12 years and shared a deep love and devotion.

Constantly under her watchful eye, I was her flock, and she was my shepherd.

For weeks after her passing, restless nights were filled with deep grief seasoned with guilt over that decision. But things shifted during one dozing, when I dreamed that God handed me a golden blonde pup with white markings.

"I will bring it to you," He said.

I awoke with peace in my heart and tear-filled eyes. Perhaps hope, perhaps faith, fueled my waiting.

My good friend, Janie Tippett, called in September, "I've found a dog for you."

Allen Voortman, who owns Pride and Joy Dairy in Granger, Washington with his wife Cheryl, had told Janie of a wild female dog who took up with his band of sheep and shepherded them about his acreage. Over time she warmed up to Allen and became a pet to his family.

He was so impressed with her, she was bred with a terrier and produced a litter of six, with one remaining puppy. Janie replied, "I know someone who needs him."

She told me the pup's story and gave me a photo of him. Golden blonde with white markings.

Three days before Christmas, I stood by Janie's snow covered driveway as Allen, a large man sporting a white beard and Santa hat, piled out of his truck and gave me a big hug.

"Wow! Hugged by Santa!" I thought.

Then he retrieved Petey and placed a wiggling cutie pie in my arms.

Allen is invited to speak around the country of his organic dairy practices which render health giving milk products. That he would bring such a special gift to me is humbling and fills me with warm gratitude.

My little pup is presently snuggled next to me, resting his head on my laptop while I wordsmith this story.

Petey is a reminder to keep open to the possibilities of what the New Year may bring. Blessed surprises, great and small, show up in the most amazing of ways.

La Grande Observer, "Wallowa Life Page," December 30, 2015.

My grandmother's sister, Aunt Carrie, is the epitome of a Southern genteel lady. She is 101 years old now, an intellectually sharp woman apprised of current events.

Think the leading actress in "Driving Miss Daisy," and you'll get the picture.

Aunt Carrie was relentless during my growing up years to transform me into a Southern Belle. More often, however, I returned home with muddy jeans and brambles in my hair.

To me, it was futile to plaster my face with makeup and douse my hair with spray. The moment I stepped outside, 100% humidity would melt me into a chemical mess.

I tried, I really tried.

She moved in with me at 98 years old, and I became her caregiver. Frequent doctor visits amused me, for they consistently remarked on how young Aunt Carrie looked, like in her late 60's- slender, upright, and with smooth tanned skin.

Her youthful appearance was the opening topic at a confab of her girlfriends who met for coffee one afternoon.

She glowed at their greetings, "Carolyn, you look so young! How do you do it?"

I summarily answered, "Bacon grease!"

I believed it. She used bacon grease to season her turnip greens, her green beans, her squash. You name it, her food was cooked with bacon grease. While my education abounded with the lessons of the harmfulness of too much fat in the diet, I couldn't dismiss the fact she was healthier than I was, though 30 years older.

She insisted I butt out of the conversation, so I left to run

errands as a sound similar to cackling hens diminished behind me.

Most of the ladies were gone by the time I returned. Aunt Carrie had enjoyed the stimulating conversation.

The next morning, she received a phone call in her room. I was putzing about in the kitchen and heard this:

"Yes, I use bacon grease a lot."

"How much? Oh, about a tablespoon."

"What?"

Then she burst out laughing.

"No, I COOK with it."

The call ended and through her giggles she recounted that one of her friends wanted to know how the bacon grease was applied to her face, "With your fingers?"

Every time I helped cook afterward, Aunt Carrie and I laughed when she reached for her special flavoring.

For me, I'll cast my chance for any youthful looks to the fresh air, real food, and mountain hikes I find in Wallowa County.

La Grande Observer, "Wallowa Life Page," January 6, 2016.

Driving Lessons

Just as Dorothy was told upon arriving in the Land of Oz, "This isn't Kansas," I repeatedly am reminded, "Katherine, this is NOT the urban South."

I am grateful for my personal council of Wallowa County elders who have time on their hands to teach me about Wallowa life. Among them are Manford and Vera Isley. How to drive in hazardous road conditions was the first lesson in my Wallowa Life education.

The problem of speeding climaxed last December. Manford and Vera invited me to their daughter's Christmas dinner in Athena. We agreed to go in my truck. He drove up there; I drove back. It was when we approached and topped Tollgate in the freezing dark that he began firmly repeating, "Slow down, Katherine."

Vera was in the back seat, probably praying.

The road was icy with a cover of light snow. I applied brakes, which gave the truck a sliding wiggle. I realized I

didn't know what to do.

"Do you want to drive?" I invited him.

"No. Just keep going," he replied.

Manford told me when to downshift and to keep a steady speed and whatever happens, don't stop. It was more than I thought I could handle, but he insisted I could do this.

The tension in the air was oppressive by the time we pulled into Joseph. We were all glad to place our feet on terra firma.

After a few days, I knocked on their door and Manford answered. I blurted out, "The other night on the way home, it became obvious I don't know how to drive on these winter roads. Would you teach me?"

With my instructor at the wheel, we headed for Imnaha. I felt like a 15 year old in Drivers Ed as he showed me how to recognize black ice. He pointed out how to approach a blind curve, with my eyes fixed on the limits of field of vision to anticipate the approach of an unseen vehicle. He explained how snow sits on ice, and how carefully I NEED TO PAY AT-TENTION.

After two weeks of practice, I asked him for a check ride. We wound through the canyons and back without my hearing, "Slow down."

My teacher does not readily hand out A's, but when Manford got out and said with a smile, "You're learning," I took that as maybe a B, and could not have been happier.

La Grande Observer, "Wallowa Life Page," January 13, 2016.

A friend and I spent much of last summer together, in what I would call an intense internship on being "A Wallowa Gal."

We headed for Imnaha one hot morning to pick blackberries. Daydreaming of buckets of juicy fruit to be gathered, I commented, "Oh, look. A snake in the road."

"Kill it!" she exploded. "Every Wallowa Gal should kill a rattlesnake!"

I snapped into a brain freeze, not immediately willing to switch my thoughts from blackberries to rattlesnakes.

She corrected me as I eased onto the road's edge, "NO! You have to run over it!" I secretly dubbed her Tawanda.

"I can't do this," I whined.

"Just drive over it slowly. Only get the head. We don't want to damage the skin."

Squish, squish. Crunch, crunch.

My breakfast wanted to get reacquainted with me.

The deed completed, I hoped to continue on to our berry picking.

"Turn around," she commanded. "We have to make sure it's dead."

So now I was driving back up the highway.

28

Same bump, bump. Same sound. I was glad we were headed in the direction of home.

"Go back. One more time."

"But I don't want to do this."

"Go back." Yes, Tawanda.

After the final pass, we pulled over and retrieved a shovel from my truck to harvest the now deceased reptile. "We need to hurry before anyone else gets it," she cautioned.

Please, God, send someone!

"Do you have a bag?" she asked.

"What for?"

"We're going to take it to Sally who owns the Tavern. She'll skin it and make a hatband for you."

"The last thing I want to wear is a snake hatband."

My eyes squeezed shut when she approached me to drop the snake into the Safeway bag held by my far extended hands.

Sally happily examined the prize stretched out on the bar. Her display of hand crafted snake skin accessories couldn't be missed.

What is it with these women? Suddenly, the South I had renounced seemed most appealing. What am I doing here?

I hurried to the door, but Tawanda caught me. "Wait! You must record this on the annual Rattlesnake Count sheet."

Katherine- 1.

As we piled into the truck, Tawanda announced, "Now you're a real Wallowa Gal!" She was so pleased.

I could only respond, "Can we pick blackberries now?"

La Grande Observer, "Wallowa Life Page," January 20, 2016.

LETTERS LOST, THEN FOUND

Last fall I told my writing mentor, Barbara, that I wanted a book project for 2016. I shared some ideas, and she recommended the story of my great-great uncle Marvin, who was killed in WWI and posthumously awarded the Distinguished Service Cross, the second highest commendation from the Army.

I asked my son, Sam, in Texas to mail me the box of family history I had left with him during my move up here. His wife mailed the contents in three separate boxes.

Only two arrived.

Sam texted me a photo of a shred of cardboard with my address on it, a notification from the postal service that the box was damaged and the items lost.

In examining the two boxes, I realized the most important things for me to complete the project were missing-the original letters between Marvin and his family, photos and news clippings I had researched and found, and the transcript of the letters I had typed fifteen years ago.

"Oh well," I regretted. "I guess God doesn't want me to write that book."

Three weeks ago, I received a voicemail from a woman named Mallory saying she had some contents I might be interested in. She didn't identify who she worked for, so I was puzzled about who she might be.

When I returned the call, she said she worked for a research company who contracts with shipping companies. When contents without a box or any identification are found during the shipping process, the items are sent to her company to research and find the proper owner.

"What do you think was in the missing box?" she asked.

"A packet of faded letters wrapped with a ribbon, old

30

photos and news clippings," hope answered. "I was going to write a book about those."

"Yes, I have those, plus the letters typed up. They are so fascinating and will make a great book!" she said happily.

After giving her the tracking number to confirm my ownership, as well as my address, I received the shipment this past Tuesday. When I pulled the top packing off, there was the packet of letters - letters which spent decades on the mantle of the family fireplace, were placed in my hands 25 years ago, traveled to Montana, back to Mississippi, to Texas, then who-knows-where, and finally here. Finally home, with me.

"Tell the story we hold," they say.

I am.

MEET MOSIE

When I told a friend I was writing a column, she advised I not talk about my pets too often. Yet I feel the need to introduce my readers to Mosie, my cat.

My husband, Richard, tamed this feral kitten over 8 years ago. I tolerated her for his sake, but I've never considered myself a cat person.

I've nothing against cats and admire my friends who adore their feline friends, but I just don't get how a person can enjoy a pet that is aloof, independent, opinionated and doesn't need anyone.

My dog, Brownie, shared the same assessment. Mosie adored Brownie and would nuzzle up to her. But Brownie would look at me and roll her eyes, "Oh, PLEASE! Get this thing away from me." Brownie was never mean to Mosie. She just wished the cat would go away.

Brownie had been ours for five years before Mosie appeared on the scene. Her domain of our family unit had been established. But all that changed when Mosie appeared.

I wanted to name her Mosaic, for she had a beautiful calico coat with a myriad of colors. But I thought that sounded dumb, so I changed it to Mosie.

I wish I'd named her Speedy, for she chose to live up to her name. She doesn't get in a hurry about anything. When she was an outside cat, I'd stand at the door and call her to come eat. She'd appear from the tree line at the back of the yard. Upon making eye contact with me, she'd mosey hyper-slow toward the house regardless of how hungry she might be. Sniff a blade of grass that had been there all summer. Stop and watch a cloud pass by. You get the picture.

It felt like she was controlling me, and I resented it. If I closed the door to rest my arm, she'd stop walking until I opened it again, even though she was still 50 yards away.

Our power struggle has a long history, but it came to a head when Brownie died.

I tried to make Mosie into my next dog, which she did NOT appreciate. No Ma'am. No walks. No cuddles. No chasing the ball.

After a few months of futile attempts, ending in a cat bite on my hand, I relented and agreed that she was the cat and in charge.

Peace has reigned ever since.

La Grande Observer, "Wallowa Life Page," February 3, 2016.

MY FRIEND HILLTON

I have a confession to make.

Remember in the movie, The Sixth Sense, the boy looks up to Bruce Willis and says, "I see dead people"?

Well, it's not that bad, but...

I see faces.

I'm not talking about the features on the front of the head of a person. I mean in nature- on mountains, in trees, in the most unlikely of places.

One in particular I see every time I drive to Enterprise from Joseph along Highway 82.

A certain morning after a snowstorm, I spotted the dark eyes and a smile embedded on the first hill of about a ton of gravel in the Moffit Construction yard.

"C'mon, Katherine. Give me a break," I chastised myself. But he couldn't be missed.

I named him Hillton, and he has become my attitude meter.

Now, when passing Eggleson Corner, I wonder, "How is Hillton doing today?"

The "face" on the south side of the gravel is more noticeable with white cover. Depending on how the wind shifts the snow, he sometimes has a frowny face. I think, "What's up with that, Hillton?"

Then I realize I myself am grumpy about something, and change my attitude before I reach my destination. But I have to say, most of the time he wears a big grin.

A circle of my friends say, "Spot it? Got it!" That is, if I'm complaining about someone else's behavior, more than likely I do the same thing. Otherwise, how would I recognize it in the first place? It took days for my toes to recover from that one.

This awareness has contributed to my usually withholding my opinion until I'm asked. (Remember "If I wanted your opinion I would have asked for it?" I finally get what that means.)

The result of my changing attitude is that my friends and I are much happier now.

Years ago, I heard, "Better to keep your mouth shut and be thought a fool, than to open it and remove all doubt." That one cracks me up.

Within the book of Proverbs is stated, "As iron sharpens iron, so a friend sharpens a friend."

I am grateful for friends like Hillton Moffit, who teach me how to live in harmony with myself and others.

My grandkids have yet to visit Wallowa County. I hope they will come soon. Hillton will be among the many they will be introduced to.

(This was a fun article that I meant to direct toward parents and grandparents to have fun with their children. Because I failed to state this clearly in the column, close friends wondered if I had lost my mind. LOL.)

La Grande Observer, "Wallowa Life Page," February 10, 2016.

Mama cows are gathered in Wallowa Valley now, and I empathize with their near bursting bellies. Bovines who spent part of the winter in the canyons have climbed to thousand foot elevations to nourish themselves and the babies inside. Some have traveled several miles, practically waddling to accommodate the extra weight they carry.

They have spent most of their pregnancy standing to graze, standing in huddles to stay warm, standing to avoid the icy ground.

I hear older women in the coffee shop discussing how beautiful the cows are. We are eager for the bouncing baby calves to be born. Mothers have a kindred heart that way.

I loved being pregnant with my children. At least the idea of it. The first three months of morning sickness weren't that appealing. My changing taste in food was a curiosity. I was going to college, and my large body swinging back and forth around campus the final weeks must have generated pity, for many students pulled up in their cars offering a ride.

That last month, I was tired.

The day before our first child was born, his daddy and I went fishing with my sister and her husband. Alongside the farm pond, I sat in a lawn chair brought for my comfort. Sister stood close by.

The guys were on the water in a john boat. Though they were fishing, they also kept their eyes on me, offering comments and suggestions to improve my chances of a catch.

The pond held smallmouth bass and bream. With each cast, I held my rod firm. At each jiggle, I yanked it up to set the hook. No fish, but the cricket was still intact.

"Must be a little bream," my husband said. "They can't always get the bait."

"Don't yank it so hard," Brother-In-Law advised.

The men began philosophizing between them as to why I couldn't catch a fish, which instilled a fierce determination within me to not be outdone. Amplified intent to react at the perfect time to reel one in led me to forget the contractions squeezing my back.

Still no luck.

"Ooh," I gasped, as the rod practically bounced out of my hands.

Questioned about why I was laughing so hard, I explained the butt of the rod had been pressed against my rotund belly; all that time the jiggling the line had been from Baby's kicks, not nibbling fish.

A Tribute to Mothers of
Teenage Boys

Oh my goodness! I had forgotten how it was. My little Petey is now "fully emerged," as veterinarian Dr. Rice described my pup's maleness. The two week process created mayhem with the following count: chewed up eyeglasses, annihilated rolls of toilet paper, and the cat is hiding in the closet. I feel like the single mother of a teenage son.

I remember when the hormones started rising in my own sons, Matthew and Sam. I often wondered if my sweet boys had been kidnapped and space aliens planted in their place.

Upon arising in the morning, they would walk past a perfectly good clean bathroom, out the kitchen door at the other end of the house, and anoint a tree in the back yard. I often scolded (to deaf ears) that they should be mindful of the privacy and decorum of living in town. I was grateful our house sat way back off the road so neighbors could not see.

Throughout the day, I'd walk in the kitchen and have to close cabinets and drawers. Every single one would be open. What were they looking for? That is, the snack cabinet made sense, but what about the cabinets holding fine china, or the one with cooking spices? I'd close them all, then go fold laundry or do yardwork. Upon returning an hour later, doors would be flung open again. Couldn't they remember that certain cabinets held nothing of interest to them? So why open them? Did they think I rearranged the contents every hour to keep them guessing? I just didn't get it.

I purchased a gallon of milk on the way home after church on a Wednesday night. Opening the refrigerator the next morning, expecting to add milk to my coffee, I'd find the jug empty, still sitting on the top shelf, with the cap lying next to it.

The kicker was whenever I asked Matthew to empty the garbage. His eyes would glaze over and he would appear distracted, as though listening to an inner voice, "YOUR-MOTHER-IS-SPEAKING-TO-YOU. HER-LIPS-ARE-MOVING. ACT-LIKE-YOU-DON'T-HEAR-AND-SHE-MIGHT-GO-AWAY."

The miracle of it all is that my boys grew up into responsible, well-adjusted men who provide for their families. So I can only hope that Petey pup will settle down after this week's surgery and mature into the dog I hope for.

SIX MONTHS

You know, this Wallowa Gal thing was supposed to be a joke in that I was a city girl from the South just trying to make her way in unfamiliar country. But now I'm not so sure...

I was helping a friend with her chickens and noticed the door to her chicken yard wouldn't shut properly. I studied the dilapidated door. At my feet lay an old bone, bleached white from sun rays, about six inches long. Very easily, I jammed the bone through a hole in the door created by a lost knothole. I cut some wire from a rotted utility pole lying on the ground nearby, made a small loop and wrapped it around a nail on the door post. Voila! The wire can easily wrap off and on the bone to open and close the door.

While visiting a friend in La Grande a few weeks ago, I noticed his storm door swaying in the wind. I saw the door closer unit was missing a bolt that secured the door piece to the frame. Scratching my head for a few minutes, I went to my truck and from the cup holder dug out a fencing nail. This remnant of last summer's project of helping friends build fence is a u- shaped nail. I inserted one of its legs into

the bolt hole, with the other side just dangling, and it's still holding.

The kicker was last month's meeting at the Observer for the freelance writers. While different topics were being discussed, my eyes could not avoid a blue cord wadded up in the corner across the room. I glanced at it throughout the meeting, wondering the whole time, "I can't understand why the Observer would need baling twine in this office." It later proved to be an unused computer cord.

Just sayin-

Be careful what you call yourself, it may come true.

Today marks six months since I began this column and writing for the Observer. I have had so much fun and have been fascinated by the people interviewed for the human interest stories. I appreciate their time for my interviews, but more than that, their kindness. I've come home with bags of vegetables from their gardens or gifts from their businesses.

But mostly I've received gifts to my heart. Watching a former drug addict mother who kisses her son before he boards the Head Start bus; observing the deep affection shared between an old muleskinner and a single mother, because his friendship and guidance restored her confidence; having a corsage pinned to my jacket by a WWII veteran and ham radio operator who makes and gives corsages to his wife. She has Alzheimer's and resides at the Senior Living Center. His companion of over 60 years doesn't know who he is, but he knows who she is, and hasn't missed a day since she began her residency. He was on day 200 when I interviewed him.

I get choked up recalling these wonderful people, who make me so grateful I get to live in Wallowa County.

La Grande Observer, "Wallowa Life Page," March 2, 2016.

WITH THE STORM

The terrific windstorm the other night really rattled my nerves. It brought back my experience during Hurricane Katrina.

In August 2005 the robotic voice of our weather radio blared, "Catastrophic Katrina. Make preparations," then described its location and estimated time of approach.

Richard and I lived about 70 miles north of the Gulf Coast of Mississippi. There was no doubt the beach land would get clobbered, but it was perplexing that our area was being forewarned. Past hurricanes had only brought us gusty winds with a splattering of rain.

But Katrina had other intentions. Once she devastated the Coast and headed northward, she paused over us. For eight merciless hours she sat and pounded us with over 100 mile per hour winds- I'll never forget the incessant roar of that gale, like a thousand freight trains.

By the time Katrina finished her work, and ambled on with a whisper of a light drizzle, the roof and ceiling of our living room were pierced with huge limbs and the floor soaked by hours of gushing rain. An immense oak tree lay atop our bed, where we had been sitting only minutes before its crashing intrusion. We crawled through the downed tree on our porch and stepped carefully over horizontal tree trunks toward the road, where we stood with our neighbors in stunned silence. Thousands of pine trees were downed, piled up as that child's game "Pick Up Sticks." The sight was beyond comprehension.

This memory kept me sleepless during the other night's tempest. But in the next day's rising sunshine, I gazed out my window toward Ruby Peak, and a rainbow's glowing colors stretched before me.

I had to run some things to a friend's house that morning. Driving along, I saw my first bluebird of Spring perched on a fence row. On my way home, another rainbow hovered in a different direction.

Noah's Bible story of old came to mind. Having weathered a harrowing storm of destruction, Noah was given a rainbow, placed by God as a promise of assurance. This symbolic arc continues to remind me that storms can be endured and rainbows wait on the other side.

Hurricane Katrina left an unnatural stark sky which lasted for months. The rainbow from that storm took eight years to appear. I found it here in Wallowa County, a land of rainbows which never stops promising hope to this Wallowa Gal.

La Grande Observer, "Wallowa Life Page," March 16, 2016.

PERFECT TIMING

I do not mean this irreverently, but the way I've seen God work sometimes, I call him "God of 'just in the nick of time.'"

For weeks I have been searching for my lost coin purse. It had belonged to my grandmother and was the one thing I asked for when she died. It also held my driver's license.

Upon rising the other morning, I gave up and planned a trip to DMV. But within two hours, I held the coin purse in my hands. The timing was perfect and reminded me of another close call.

In 2009, my husband Richard and I had been battling his lung cancer for months. When told it had spread to his brain, we fell into numb resignation.

I found him one morning with an open Bible in his hands. I was very involved in church activities, but he never was interested in joining me.

He looked up. "I think there's something in here I need to know," he said pensively.

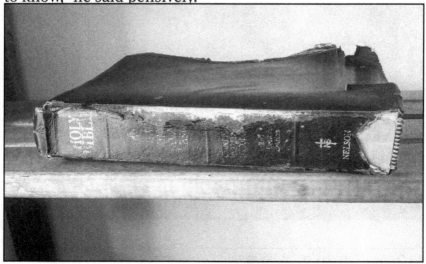

"Would you like me to arrange a Bible study? I'm too close to be objective," I responded.

Being acquainted with some of my church friends, he was open to their coming over. At the second visit of reading and conversations about Jesus of Nazareth, the story of salvation and forgiveness hit its mark. Richard's face brightened.

"That is so simple!" he exclaimed.

After his baptism, he was different. Richard always had cussed like a sailor because, well, he once was a sailor. But no such language now. His parents died when he was a boy, and from his stories of them throughout our marriage, it was easy to see how much he missed them. But now he looked forward to seeing them again.

He had lived a rough life in foster homes and had run away, eventually joining the military where he spent most of his life. He had done things in Vietnam that, though necessary, he regretted.

Now, peace.

Eight days after his baptism, Richard was bedridden with the brain tumor having its way.

It was the serenity he carried those final days I'll remember more than the cancer battle. Some might say the fight was over at his death, but honestly, I think it was over when he said, "That is so simple."

He dodged a bullet of eternal significance and won the last war. Just in the nick of time.

La Grande Observer, "Wallowa Life Page," March 23, 2016.

THIS TOWN IS NOT OUR OWN
PART 1

I'm writing this behind drawn curtains, because, well... I'm going to reveal a dark secret about Joseph town.

Tourists are often awed by the majestic mountains just outside of town and enamored with the sidewalk shopping along Main Street. The friendliness of the locals enchants the visitors, resulting in the comment, "I want to live here!"

That's all well and good, but full disclosure must be given about what goes on in the obscure neighborhoods tucked behind the charming storefronts of downtown Joseph.

I'm talking about the gangs that have taken over the streets, The Guardians and The Nomads.

The Guardians are the abundant gangs of deer who intrude their way onto any property they wish. Mayor Sands and the council members may think they are the decision makers in this town, but The Guardians call the shots.

The Guardians use extortion to finance protective services. It may cost some tulips or apples from your tree, or the use of a fine lawn for a poop depository, but you will pay.

Some may say, "Just use your gun to dispose of them." But The Guardians have back up. I guarantee, if it is discovered that one of these deer has been shot, even if the meat is donated to the Food Bank at Community Connections, complaints will be raised against the shooter and his family. Worst of all, they will be gossiped about for months.

"Remember what ol' Joe did with that buck on Mill Street, dontcha know," a coffee drinker at the Cheyenne Café will bring up. Without further discussion, others around the table will shake their heads in disgust, for they all DO know what Joe did.

The Guardians use bullying as their modus operandi. One time a doe I've named Daisy entered my yard as the matriarch of her entourage of younger does. She stomped her foot several times at my dog, insisting it pay homage to her. Then she jerked her head around and chased the other does away. In a regal stance, her head held high, she marched on to my neighbor's yard.

I tell you, she thinks she owns the place.

The Guardians by name imply that they are protectors, so it raises the question, "From whom?"

That would be the Nomads. But my word budget forces us to wait until next week for the description of these terrorists and the gang wars.

La Grande Observer, "Wallowa Life Page," March 30, 2016.

THIS TOWN IS NOT OUR OWN
PART 2

Last week I broke the news about the gang wars between The Guardians and The Nomads. The Guardians are the herds of deer who use the extortion of tulips, daffodils and public potty privileges to protect the citizens of Joseph.

The question is now raised, "From whom are The Guardians protecting us?"

That would be The Nomads.

These are the scads of California Quail who roam the housing territory, using our paved roads and flying our skies without one bit of licensing.

Yes, they seem like innocent little birds, with sweet sounds of chirping as they pass by.

From personal experience, however, I can attest that they are militant terrorists.

I am awakened on mornings with "Reveille" outside my window, with the quail cocks crowing. They are hidden in camouflaged barracks among the thick limbs of a nearby spruce tree. But I see their outlines scurrying among the branches, backlit by the rising sun.

When they ramble along the street out front, there is always the one who mounts the peak of the large rock in my front yard. The Crowned One announces, "I rule!"

I have a tall cedar tree next to where I park my car. In the dark of night, as I'm unloading my things to bring in the house, I'll hear a rustle and a whisper of a cluck up in the dense tree, as though they are saying, "Shhh. Everybody, QUIET, so she won't know we're here."

Having forgotten what has happened on numerous occasions in the past, I smile, "Oh, the quail are here. How nice."

At my most unsuspecting moment, they explode out of the tree and drop over the fence to my neighbor's yard. I try to still my palpitating heart while picking up groceries scattered about me.

"They got me," I mutter. "AGAIN!"

Last fall a fruit tree across the street attracted a small group of Guardians. While they enjoyed crisp apples, a fawn spotted The Nomads in my front yard. The curious youth slowly came across the street for investigation. The Crowned One spotted him and led his minions on a frontal attack that pushed the youngster back, and The Guardians moved on.

I question the veracity of The Guardians' protection I pay for. I check for clearance before I leave the house. I just wanted any newcomers to be well-informed of the gangs that hold us captive in Joseph, Oregon.

La Grande Observer, "Wallowa Life Page," April 6, 2016

"Colston would like to schedule FT with you," read the text from my daughter-in-law, Angela. Seven year old Colston, my oldest grandchild, and I have become adept at Facetime. This video phone service is a vital link between my sons' children and me, allowing me to stay in Wallowa County. Without contact via Facetime, I don't think I could endure the distance between us.

I bought my IPad last fall and we had a difficult learning curve- mostly that we have to schedule our calls around his busy family life. I would attempt to connect with him with no answer, but an explaining text would soon come from his mother that Colston was studying.

Other times I'd come home and find that I had missed a call from Colston. I'd get choked up with tears because he wanted to talk to me and I wasn't home. After about a month of this we eventually connected and giggled, "Finally!"

"This is the spaceship I built for you," I hear his voice as the video transits each week's creation of his made with Legos. Then he explains each part that, thankfully, I'm somewhat familiar with because they include Star Wars characters.

"Did you design it yourself or follow instructions?" GranKK asks.

"I did it myself."

"How smart is that?" And I really mean it, for he is thoughtful about the meaning and placement of each piece.

His younger siblings, Annabella and Stanton want to talk, and I speak loud enough for them to hear, "We're going to take turns, and it's Colston's turn right now." I hear them leave the room.

I enjoy seeing how Colston thinks and his ever growing looks. He has a gappy smile right now, because some of his teeth are missing and the larger ones are coming in. He is getting tall like my older son Matthew. I get to examine any scrapes and hear the accompanying stories.

This is the child that wanted me to play the game "Memory" with him when he was three. After setting up the game, he turned to me with his hands on his hips, and in all seriousness said, "Now, the first thing you need to always remember is that I go first."

I restrained my mirth until after the game, then went outside for a big laugh.

Yes, Colston, you are right. You are always first in GranKK's heart.

La Grande Observer, "Wallowa Life Page," April 13, 2016.

I volunteered for Divide Camp for about a year and saw for myself the direct benefits veterans gain who visit this encampment.

I was present in the fall of 2014 when a group of three vets, Marshall, Aaron and Corey, came up for a long weekend. There was no hunting or fishing trip scheduled. They only wanted to spend time at camp. I anticipated that they would sit around and chat or read- like a mini-vacation. But soon after arriving, they were asking Julie, the director, what they could do to help around camp. Marshall and Corey got busy with handyman projects. Aaron moved a stack of wood.

I pitched in and helped Aaron with the wood. I asked how had he learned of Divide Camp. He said from another vet, but he was wary at first.

"There are so many so-called organizations out there saying they want to help veterans, but they exploit them and are frauds. I did a lot of research on the Internet about Divide Camp, and talked to others. I saw it is the real deal," he explained.

Divide Camp has no connections to the Wounded Warrior Project, which has been in the news recently for its mismanagement of donations which landed in the pockets of high-salaried employees before it reached the veterans it is supposed to serve. Divide Camp has no paid personnel and is overseen by a volunteer Board, consisting of volunteer veterans and civilians.

As a volunteer, I personally saw how conscientious Director Julie Wheeler manages the DC budget- every penny spent is with the well-being of the veterans in mind.

While serving Divide Camp, the opportunity arose for me to write full time. My heart was torn because I love the

mission of Divide Camp, "Helping them heal, one warrior at a time." Yet I felt like I had to pursue my writing.

Divide Camp's fundraising banquet is April 30. Tickets are for sale online with a credit card at www.dividecamp.org or at the Blonde Strawberry, the Bookloft, and the Sports Corral. In La Grande they may be purchased at All Air Heating and Air Conditioning. Sponsorships help cover the overhead costs and provide tickets to local veterans.

In the future I will share personal stories about what I observed at Camp and how it helps veterans. For now, I hope you will attend the banquet and hear their own stories.

La Grande Observer, "Wallowa Life Page," April 20, 2016.

I choose not to have television service because of the news channels. B. W. L. (Before Wallowa Life) I had noticed the news anchors, especially Brian Williams of NBC, gained too much pleasure in telling me the worst news possible. Brian would tell me what happened, what I should think about what happened, and that I should be upset about what happened.

I guess Jack Webb of Dragnet personifies the kind of news listener I am, "The facts, ma'am. Just give me the facts."

I didn't need someone telling me what to think of the news... I can think for myself.

I didn't need encouragement to get disturbed about the news. I'm all about peace.

After spending 25 minutes telling me how screwed up the world was, Mr. Williams would wrap it up in a pretty package with the closing segment "Making a Difference."

So my "watching the news" experience felt like this: "We're all about to be nuked. You and your family are going to die.

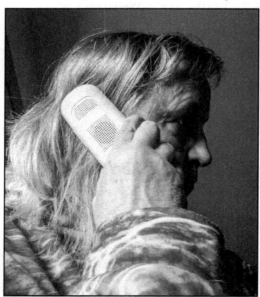

But the good news is a little girl saved a butterfly today."

I simply don't need that.

Amazingly, I discover what's newsworthy just by being out and about.

"How are your kids?" a friend will ask me at the post office, her worried look signifying something may be wrong.

"Ok, I guess. Why do you ask?"

"Yesterday Texas had hailstones the size of baseballs. Someone was killed when one came through the windshield."

She doesn't know what part of Texas or that the state is as large as the universe, so the storm could have happened anywhere. I return home and thankfully learn on the Internet it was 300 miles north of my children.

I could call my sons about this, but this is how those conversations go...

Me: "How's it going?"

Sam: "OK."

"I heard y'all had storms."

"Yeah." Long silence as I wait for further explanation. Nothing.

"Are y'all okay?"

"Yeah."

Long silence...

"What part of the state were they in?"

"I don't know." (Not "I'll have to check and see.")

His brother, Matthew, is even worse.

The lack of verbal effusion from these two 30-somethings astounds me, because when I go for a visit, they are constantly on the phone.

Notwithstanding, by the time you read this, I will be immersed within my family, including six week old grandchild (#6) whose middle name is Katherine.

Now THAT'S news worth reporting.

La Grande Observer, "Wallowa Life Page," April 27, 2016.

WHAT IS THE WILD?

For the first few days of my visit, I had Sam's two boys to myself. Daily, I invited Silas (4) and Tate (3) to my bedroom where my smaller traveling bag held surprises in two outside pockets, one larger than the other.

"Tate gets to unzip the big zipper," I instructed. "Then Silas can open the other one."

Tate got a different book each day. We would sit on the couch for me to read, then it was Silas' turn.

The first morning, he pulled out a kaleidoscope I had purchased at Copper Creek in Joseph. He loved it! Silas is my "imagination boy," and after each turn, he handed it to me.

"Look, GranKK!"

After the next day's book reading, Silas retrieved two pussy willow stems. "What is this?" he asked.

"Pussy willows. They grow in the wild."

"What's the wild?"

I froze at a loss for words. My mouth felt too small to describe where I live- the vastness, the beauty, the rawness of it all.

His blue eyes patiently waited for me to answer.

"The wild is where there are mountains and rivers and forests and the sky is big. Animals live where there are no people."

"No people?"

"No people."

He stroked the soft buds. "I want to put these in a vase."

Tate trailed behind us to the kitchen. He'd been guarded with me, not knowing me as well as Silas.

Their mother told me where to find a small vase. It was more of a small glass bowl which did not allow the sticks to stand upright.

"Let's go outside and find a rock to hold them up," I decided.

We went outside and could not find one single rock, not a piece of gravel anywhere in the well-manicured lawn and cul-de-sac. I was dumbfounded. I'm from Wallowa County where there is nothing but rocks of all sizes. It was beyond my comprehension.

"How do you raise boys without rocks?" I wondered.

Back in the house, I requested a toy car.

Silas came back with a race car. I dropped it in the vase, and arranged the stems just right.

Seeing this success, Tate instantly wrapped both arms around my leg and hugged me.

GranKK had scored.

The next day an ocean green rock from one of my hikes was the surprise, and all was right with the world.

Boys need rocks. Wild ones.

LET'S GO FOR A WALK

"The earth laughs in flowers." Ralph Waldo Emerson

If this is true, Wallowa County is having giggle fits.

This is my second Spring at this residence and my lilacs are stunning. Their heady fragrance nearly knocks me down when I step out the door. Most are lavender and white, but some are a deep purple that a neighbor says is the old-fashioned kind.

I think she's right. Last week I was wandering around the pioneer cemetery next to the Joseph Airport where a clump of similar purple lilacs is nestled in the center. Seeing some headstones suffocating under the thick growth, I pushed my way through and found dates of death in the late 1800's. I don't know if lilacs can live over 100 years, but their thick trunks showed they'd been there a very long time.

A drive to the head of Wallowa Lake in the afternoon is problematic in that it's hard to keep my eyes on the road. The water on my right is mirror-smooth. On my left shimmer the sunshine yellow blossoms of arrowleaf balsalmroot carpeting the East Moraine. They seem to go forever.

I let Petey have a good run at the Little Alps park while I ramble around. The river is up, and the rush of tumbling waters echoes up the mountain walls into the trees, making me feel like I'm in the river itself, though not getting wet.

The upturned faces of forget-me-nots greet me as I near the river bed. Squirrels scold Petey, enticing him to a chase. I laugh at his run which is randomly interrupted by a springy bounce that makes him airborne. The squirrels always win.

A side stream has been created by the elevated river level, and I cross on a weathered log. Since I moved to Wallowa County and have made several hikes, my balance has improved immensely from several log-crossings. This skill is a necessity if I'm to live near so many trails.

I'm amazed to find pale wallflowers poking up between the river rocks. I visited this spot countless times during the winter, never suspecting these lemon-colored surprises were underneath the snow and ice, waiting for Spring.

Calling Petey, we head toward the bridge on the Chief Joseph Trail. Pink fairy slippers and yellow wood violets ornament the side of my path.

Tears well up inside- I am so thankful I get to live here.

La Grande Observer, "Wallowa Life Page," May 11, 2016.

THE PRICE OF FORGETTING IS
TOO HIGH

At past Memorial Day ceremonies conducted by members of the V. F. W. and American Legion Posts, I've often wondered why there are only a handful of Post members present, with a scattering of public citizens.

"They remember," the answer comes.

"But, since all Americans experience freedom, aren't we too called upon to remember the price our freedom extracted?" I ask.

To me, Memorial Day is about remembering the one who signed a blank check to the United States, guaranteeing the withdrawal of his life if necessary. And it has been necessary, thousands and thousands of times, as evidenced by the many flags marking graves throughout our country on Memorial Day.

My Vietnam veteran husband Richard found Memorial Day difficult. That is, he would watch on TV the different ceremonies across the U. S. to commemorate the fallen soldiers. At

each one, he would wipe his eyes as "Taps" was played.

"Gets to me every time," he'd gruffly say. Yet he wouldn't turn off the TV. He needed to remember.

"Taps" was originally known as a lullaby, and was incorporated into the military during the

Civil War. It was simply a call at the end of a soldier's day for rest, along the same lines as "Reveille" was blasted each morning to start a soldier's day.

It took on greater meaning when it was assigned to military funerals.

The lyrics were written by Horace Lorenzo Trim and begin with:

"Day is done, gone the sun

From the lakes, from the hills, from the sky

All is well, safely rest

God is nigh..."

For me to go on as Richard's widow, I can only think of him as safely resting on that hillside at Willamette National Cemetery with Mt. Hood gazing upon him from a distance. Richard now rests from the combat nightmares I would have to calm him down from in the darkest hour of night. He now rests from hypervigilance, where he quickly ascertained the exit to any public facility we visited and always had to sit facing the door of a restaurant. He rests from the combat bullet wound which pierced his leg. And he rests from the lung cancer which spread to his brain, caused by exposure to toxic fumes and chemicals during his military service.

For the price of freedom, what does it cost us to remember? Only the effort to set aside time to drive to your local cemetery and spend not more than 30 minutes at the posting of the flag while "Taps" is played. Each name engraved on a headstone with a small flag by its side will speak from the grave, "I fought for that flag. I fought for freedom's sake."

We must remember the price of freedom, for the price of forgetting is even higher.

Rest in peace, my love. I will always remember.

La Grande Observer, "Wallowa Life Page," May 18, 2016.

To me, what is so wonderful about Wallowa County is that there are as many different ways to enjoy her as there are people.

Last week, on a drizzly misty day, I was driving to La Grande. When I got to Minam, there were cows walking the railroad track downriver. Cowboys in yellow slickers and working dogs were easing the mothers and their calves along the rails, their bellows joining the song of the river echoing up the canyon walls.

I couldn't wrap my mind around the spectacle of a cattle drive on a rail line. Yet it made sense, for the Excursion Train wasn't running that day. That short route gave access to the open slope where, over a hundred years ago, pioneers climbed with their wagons and stock over the top of Smith Mountain. From there, they could see miles of the verdant grass of Wallowa Valley which became their livelihood and remains such today for many growers. I felt like I was watching history, still in the making.

I was standing alongside the now high and swift Wallowa River, photographing the cattle on the other side, when two rubber rafts drifted quickly by.

The next morning when I opened my curtain, a student pilot was flying out of Joseph Airport. Later that day I was driving on a back road in the county, enjoying the new growth of hay fields, and I passed some bicyclists. That evening I went for a short hike by the Wallowa River and stepped over the evidence of horseback trail riders ahead of me.

At the Sports Corral I joined a line to obtain hunting and fishing licenses. The main topic of conversations among my girlfriends are what stage of planting their gardens are in.

Two friends and I snatched an afternoon up on the Divide, just to see the wildflowers. The landscape up on top

blanketed with wildflowers with snow-peaked mountains not too far away is astounding.

R. V.'s coming through Joseph are becoming more numerous now, headed for campgrounds located throughout the county. Boats kick up wakes on the glass smooth lake while families picnic alongside the water which provides sustenance for us all.

I remember in my junior high history class, that the attraction of the land that was to become the United States of America was the vast array of natural resources stretching from shore to shore. To have so much within one country governed by its own people makes us the richest place of all.

As a young girl in Girl Scouts, I enjoyed the catchy rendition of "This Land is Your Land" we sang around the campfire, though I didn't understand the significance of the lyrics originally penned by Woody Guthrie 13 years before I was born.

Wallowa County is a microcosm of how this land is shared and enjoyed, as Guthrie well wrote, "This land was made for you and me."

La Grande Observer, "Wallowa Life Page," May 25, 2016.

For a few weeks now, I've been seeing Forget-Me-Not flowers mingling in the grasses at the head of Wallowa Lake. Tucked here and there, their little blue faces seem to say, "Don't forget me!"

Yet it's more than the flowers that are bringing that message to mind. This time last year, I had to have my Australian Shepherd "Brownie" put down. As I now sit before my laptop, I still find it difficult to talk about our time together.

I was running errands and on a whim, stopped at the local shelter, which was a large compound of concrete kennels. From the back of the last enclosure, I heard a clanging and walked around to investigate. A gray spaniel pup shared a cage with a small brown companion. The spaniel was scrambling about the floor, and I soon saw that it was running around snatching up dry kibble bits. The brown pup accidently spilled food from the metal bowl when she put her front paw in.

At least I thought it was accidental. I continued to watch and realized she repeatedly tipped the bowl on purpose. She wanted its contents to herself, and would scatter some to keep the spaniel occupied and away from the main dish.

I cracked up laughing, "You smart little thing!" An attendant handed her to me, and she fit just right on my arm and in my heart.

After setting her down I was asked, "What are you going to name her?"

Her coat was a deep chocolate brown, like a panful of brownies. This reminded me of Brownie Girl Scouts I had enjoyed as a little girl.

"Brownie," I said to myself out loud, and she came to me with her stub of a tail wagging.

Her cleverness was nothing but joy to me. She loved to

learn, and actually taught me many things- mostly how to play. Her version of "Fetch" went like this: I would throw the Frisbee. She would run to where it landed, then sit by it, regardless of how many times I told her to bring it to me. I would finally relent, walk to her and throw the Frisbee again. She would run to it and wait, again. All over the yard we'd go, and I'm just now realizing who was really doing the fetching.

When we moved here, I would take her for walks and became known as "Brownie's Mom." She was strikingly beautiful and no matter where I went, passersby would stop and talk to her while totally ignoring me.

Last year, I could have let her declining mobility from old age drag on. But she would give an embarrassed look when she couldn't walk anymore, or had an incontinent moment, or a bad coughing spell. I simply couldn't let her end be any less than dignified.

After her passing, I wrote a poem titled "Psalm 23 for Brownie."

She was some kind of dog.

PSALM 23 FOR BROWNIE

By Katherine Stickroth

Brownie was my shepherd
I wanted no other dog
On our hikes along Imnaha River we rested in green meadows
At evening we sat by the still waters of Wallowa Lake
Her companionship restored my soul
When I didn't know which trail to take home,
She led me on the right path, no matter what
Because I was hers, to watch over and protect

Yes, though I've walked through the valleys of loss
I couldn't give up
For Brownie was with me
I looked into her deep amber eyes
And when she wiggle-tailed
She comforted me

She endeared herself to strangers for she greeted all as her friends
Her gentle licks anointed me with her love

My heart runs over with deep affection and gratitude for my good
shepherd
Goodness and mercy followed me all the days we had together

For on the way home, she
trailed behind me
She always had my back

Brownie will dwell
in my heart
Forever

La Grande Observer, "Wallowa Life Page," June 1, 2016.

THE WINDS OF CHANGE
ARE BLOWING

It's been windy here lately. One of my Wallowa County elders says the winds always indicate change. And sure enough, a recent policy change at the Observer does not provide for me to continue this column.

I went back to my first column, dated September 2, 2015 and read that I invited you for a ride as I explore the "tongue in cheek" moniker placed on me, "A Wallowa Gal." Each week I looked forward to sharing my experiences here and the lessons learned from them. Within the canyons and spread across the broad vistas of my new home are fascinating people, each with a story to tell, and I was privileged to write articles about some.

I'm grateful for Andrew Cutler, editor, who gave me the opportunity to write for the Observer. I have a special affection for the Wallowa Life editor Cherise Kaechele, a bright, intelligent young woman with a teacher's heart, who patiently taught me not only the nuances of writing for a newspaper, but explained what a "selfie" is.

The staff always had a friendly greeting for me, but maybe it was more for Petey. They loved to see him when we dropped by.

Yet there's still more to learn about being a Wallowa Gal. I'm blogging now at awallowagal.com if you'd like to continue the ride.

This past weekend, a friend invited me to stay at her cabin while she was out of town. I stopped just before the creek crossing. "We just gotta do it," I firmly told my dog Petey and Mosie Cat, whose eyes were fixed on me.

We made it fine.

I split wood before a soft rain descended for hours that afternoon. The previous weekend, I had attended Flora Days and from observing Vanessa Thompson with her cook stove, I was able to use the one in the cabin for warmth and food preparation.

The creek always gurgled nearby, and I wondered if it had risen any with the previous day's rain.

"Can't do anything about it anyway," so I stopped worrying.

An evening walk found me gazing upon a magnificent hillside of wildflowers. What a lovely bouquet to end the day with.

I went to bed with a good tired. My intent in going there was to do a lot of writing and reading. But mostly I found mindless chores to do. I enjoyed the labor of it, and it was a pleasure to just be in the moment, doing the next right thing. I haven't slept that sound in a long time.

I packed us up the next frosty morning and plunged through the creek all right. And as I remember that weekend, I think I might be gaining on being a Wallowa Gal.

~ ~ ~

With my association with the La Grande Observer now ended, I contacted Rob Ruth, editor of Wallowa County's Chieftain newspaper. Would he consider publishing "A Wallowa Gal" column?

He agreed, and I continued relating my stories of Wallowa County life.

La Grande Observer, "Wallowa Life Page," June 22, 2016.

A Gardening Gal

I am grateful for the opportunity to wear my Wallowa Gal hat again. I began this column last year in another publication and had fun sharing stories of my new life in Wallowa County.

I was jokingly dubbed "A Wallowa Gal," by a local friend here who noticed cow manure on my vehicle. (I blog at awallowagal.com, where my naming and other stories are under the tab "Past Columns". Photos associated with this column are also posted on the blog. Comments are welcome.)

My first summer here I was graced to become friends with an older couple who let me help them garden. It quickly became apparent to the three of us that I knew nothing about gardening.

I was ready to jump in and start planting, but they were more interested in preparing the soil. Mostly I sat in the dirt digging up "dambuttonweeds" and tossing rocks that had worked their way up during the winter.

One time I dug up a rusty nail. When I held it up, I was told it was necessary to add iron in the vegetables.

"Really?" I asked with naïve enthusiasm, returning it to the earth.

When I looked up and saw the twinkle in his eyes, he said, "No..." and we both laughed that I had a lot to learn.

After frantically attacking the dirt with a shovel,

I soon learned from watching them to be careful, slow and methodical.

They had that soil groomed so perfectly it looked like an earthly carpet. Finally, I was allowed to help plant, which began another chapter in gardening. Seeds are to be gently planted, not dumped.

I made myself available to help weed during the growing season, but I wasn't invited too often, because they spent most of their time saying, "Watch your step, Katherine" as a carrot head recovered from my boot.

It was such a pleasure when I visited them and left with zucchini, beets and onions. Each meal of the vegetables I had helped with was more delicious than any I had prepared from store-bought.

At the beginning of my now third summer here, I prepared two small raspberry patches in my back yard. I was advised by my elders to fence it because of the deer.

The typical busyness of Wallowa County summer life tumbled upon me, and I decided to just chance it. One of my elders came by to inspect. The chew marks on my poor raspberries were brought to my attention. (My quick glances as I had run in and out of the house had me believing my raspberries were very slow in growing.)

With big rocks, old lumber, chicken wire and a staple gun, I built what at best can only be called a contraption for my raspberries.

Well-trained gardeners might raise an eyebrow upon inspecting this, but my explanation is the deer are so amused they forget about the raspberries and leave laughing.

It's amazing how well my raspberry stalks are growing. Like them, I too am establishing roots here.

Wallowa County Chieftain, "A Wallowa Gal," July 28, 2016.

HOME REMEDIES

Among the many enjoyments of living in Wallowa County are my friendships with people descended from pioneer stock. Because they are rich in common sense, I benefit from their wisdom.

My Wallowa County elders are agile and active, quick-minded and smart- how I aspire to be well into my 80's. Many conversations center around growing and preparing their own food. Therefore, my health has improved a hundredfold by following their eating habits and trying out home remedies.

One winter day, as I was visiting some friends, they asked me about the Band-Aids on each of my fingers. Upon hearing of my dried and cracked cuticles, they suggested I coat my fingers with lard. My questions led to a demonstration on "rendering lard" and I was gifted with a jar of the prized substance.

Before bed that night, I applied the hog fat, even covering my entire hands because it felt so good. After carefully crawling between the bed linens so as not to rub it off, I fell asleep ignoring the fact that I smelled like bacon in a frying pan.

The only problem from this experiment was that an hour later I woke up to my cat and dog licking my fingers.

I wore gloves the rest of night, and sure enough, it worked.

Another condition that required attention might be a sensitive subject for some, but because October is Breast Cancer Awareness Month, I'm going to share my story.

This past July, on my first day at the Outpost writer's workshop offered by Fishtrap, my breasts became fire engine red and very, very painful. An emergency room visit that night armed me with antibiotics, yet when I returned home from Outpost at the end of the week, things had not improved.

Breast cancer is normally thought of as only determined by the discovery of a lump. But I remembered Inflammatory Breast Cancer (IBC), the fast-growing kind with no tumor. Researching on the Internet, my condition matched IBC symptoms and photos.

Flooded with memories of my husband's fight with cancer, a terrible fear drove me to several doctors for a definitive diagnosis.

The appointment with Doctor #4 led to a recommendation for a sports bra. She thought I had said a RIDERS workshop (a horseback riding clinic), not a WRITERS workshop. When I explained I was only holding a pen, we broke into giggle fits. She referred me to a surgeon for a biopsy, and a close friend arranged for me to see a breast specialist in Boise. This physician readily diagnosed mastitis.

What? It had been 34 years since I had nursed a baby.

Tears of relief... then joy, pure joy. Friends at home had been holding their breath, praying for me. Upon leaving the clinic, I immediately called them with the good news.

And being from Wallowa County, where so many of my friends are ranch women, by the time I got off the phone, I

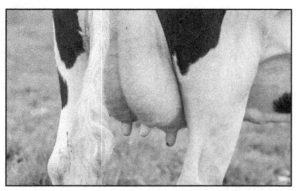

had five offers of Bag Balm for my udders.

I promptly bought my own, and can personally attest to the value of home remedies.

Wallowa County Chieftain, "A Wallowa Gal," September 22, 2016.

"BUSY" IS HOW WE ROLL

A friend texted me recently, apologizing for not getting in touch sooner because she had been so busy.

I responded, "'Busy' is how we roll in Wallowa County."

I'm learning how to hunt and had a whitetail doe tag. As we drove around, a friend who has lived and breathed this Wallowa Land for decades spent a lot of time teaching me about the habits of deer and their movement during the fall. Of how they are driven by their need for water and feed, and how weather conditions are a big factor.

We mostly stayed on the backcountry roads. I didn't always know where I was. That is, I couldn't show you on a map, but when we would top out on a ridge, I could make a mental note, "Okay, Finley Buttes are over there." Or "There's the Divide." Chief Joseph Mountain was my main bearing point.

Interspersed in these stories were comments about my driving. "Slow down, Katherine." By day 5 I wasn't hearing that so often.

I never realized how much hunting can keep a person busy. Hours and hours are devoted to scouting. Nor did I realize how much work comes with success. The field dressing, loading, hanging, then cutting and packaging of meat- lots of work.

Much was taught to me, some was learned- mostly that I don't have any idea what I'm doing most of the time. At least that keeps me teachable. And a great deal could be said on the value of a patient friend.

My most favorite time of this hunting season was one afternoon, somewhere, we were scouting on foot. He showed me tracks of deer and elk who had just walked that trail. I heard the pounding hoof beats of departing elk, just before he told me to sniff and smell the musky odor of those elk.

We hiked for about a mile, gaining on elevation. After the sun dropped over the mountains, we turned back. I was watching for tracks again, then looked up and stopped.

It was a "freeze-frame" moment.

I heard the creek murmuring below us, hidden within a velvet carpet of ponderosa pine which was sprinkled with bright yellow tamarack spires. Beneath a near full moon, the Seven Devils were gold-tinted against a clear blue sky. My friend was still walking ahead of me. Just then a hawk rose to become airborne, banking in flight to where its white underside was fully exposed just above my friend's white cap.

The beauty of this wildness, of the freedom to be here, and this time with a treasured friend all hit me at once and caught my breath away.

At the end of my hunting season, I was pretty tired. I soon forgot that fatigue. In a few months, the meat will be gone, and I'll forget about that while next summer I eat mostly garden gleanings.

Yet never, ever will I forget the image of that captured moment in Wallowa County. I like where "busy" takes me.

Wallowa County Chieftain, "A Wallowa Gal," October 28, 2016.

A CHRISTMAS HOPE

I have a faded color photo of a Christmas tree with gobs of wrapped presents underneath. Far more presents than my poor parents could afford.

Christmas had been approaching for my parents and their five children ages three years and younger. An unexpected pair of twin girls had been born three months earlier. In the first week of December 1960, one of the babies died of SIDS. How did my parents provide that kind of a Christmas for us that year with such a tragedy on their shoulders?

They didn't.

It was our neighbors who came through. We lived in a cookie-cutter neighborhood outside of Washington D. C. - houses looked the same, working fathers wore the same dark suits, stay-at-home mothers wore Jackie O. look-alike sweaters. In the evenings parents would gather for cocktails at each other's homes while their children played dodgeball in the street and at other times had crabapple wars- all the same.

What wasn't the same is that at my parent's darkest hour other families made sure my younger siblings and I had a Christmas. It wasn't that it would have mattered to us children. We were young enough to have gone through Christmas and not known whether Santa came or not.

Those neighbors simply did the right thing, and their kindness gave my parents hope that someone cared about them. Though I wasn't aware of this circumstance at the time, holding this photo impacts me today.

I listen to people I care about in despair about the election results, who see no hope with the new president-elect. And while I have my own opinions about these times at hand, I truly believe it's all going to work out.

It's out of my hands, really. So rather than going global

with my musings, I bring it back home, back to Wallowa County. I had never seen how interdependence works until I moved here. How independent people with polarizing political beliefs will together make sure an elderly neighbor has enough firewood to stay warm. Not government agencies, but people helping people. I see mysterious bags of groceries appearing on the steps of a home where the father has just lost his job. No SNAP card can do that.

Soon after I moved here, I was commenting to a new friend how generous Wallowa Countians are. She laughed,

"We may talk about you behind your back, but by God, if you need something, we'll be the first ones to help you." I smiled all the way home, "If that isn't a picture of the human condition..."

We can be so imperfect, but when it comes right down to it, I believe there is goodness in each of us. The worst alcoholic can have a moment of holding the door open for someone. A homeless woman will share one of her few crackers with a stray cat that tags along.

The most unlikely of people can do extraordinary things. Whether it's the story of kindness and generosity in a faded Christmas photo, or the story of an unlikely mother, in an unlikely stable, having an unlikely son who brings peace on earth and goodwill toward all- however it's told, I believe hope is still with us.

Merry Christmas, everyone.

Wallowa County Chieftain, "A Wallowa Gal," December 2, 2016.

A Reason to Read

During the blazing summer of 2013, I worked as a trail guide for the Tram, taking visitors around the top of Mt. Howard and telling stories about Wallowa County. One group of women from San Francisco, about my age, huffed and puffed along.

At one break, one woman asked me, "Where does everyone go in the winter?"

"What do you mean?"

"Where does everyone go when they evacuate because of the snow?"

A picture of what this would look like flashed through my mind, and it was all I could do to keep a straight face.

"Well, we don't leave. We put on more clothes, make sure we have good tires, and we're good to go."

The five women stared at me in disbelief.

One exclaimed, "I could never do that."

I thought to myself, "You're probably right." But I said, "It's do-able."

With two feet of snow outside my window, I buck up by repeating, "This place is not for sissies, that's for sure."

Yet winter in Wallowa County is more than dealing with snow. We build extra time for shopping at Safeway, because we're sure to run into someone we know which leads into an hour long conversation. Amidst bananas and potatoes, with people walking around us, we catch up on any kind of news, grateful to see a different face, to hear a different voice.

And activities continue to draw people out of their snow burrows, such as Fishtrap's The Big Read event. This year's book selection, "The Things They Carried" by Tim O'Brian is a work of fiction about Vietnam. Snowbound, I'm reading it now and quite frankly, I find there's a lot of truth in his words. I've heard similar stories from my husband Richard and other Vietnam vets I've met over the years.

As a member of The Big Read committee, I appreciate the sensitivity I've seen by other members and find it remarkable that decades beyond the Vietnam conflict, the topic continues to raise emotional responses. What I enjoy about The Big Read is that with so many locals reading the same book, conversations are generated that might not take place otherwise.

"Where were you during Vietnam?"

Some people were in combat there. Some were parents anxiously awaiting word from their sons. Some were wives, wondering if their husbands would make it home. Some were children, confused because their father didn't act the same as before he left. Some were hippies rebelling against The Establishment.

As remote as Wallowa County is, it was affected by Vietnam. Old timers have stories of Vietnam veterans and hippies of that era drifting in, desiring to find a new life. These "newcomers" shifted the culture of Wallowa County, bringing new ideas, new ways of doing things.

I encourage readers to watch for Fishtrap's calendar of events for The Big Read and come when you can. Among them will be a discussion by a panel of veterans who have read the book. A photo display "Exit Wounds" will be on exhibit at Divide Camp Headquarters in Joseph, and then in Wallowa, with the photographer giving a presentation. "Good Morning, Vietnam!" will be shown at the OK. These are open to the public- veterans of all eras and citizens, young and old.

By reading "The Things They Carried," and attending the events, perhaps we will learn what we each have carried since the tornadic '60's which circled around Vietnam.

And understand.

FLYING IN WALLOWA COUNTY

What does a gal do as a pilot lifts his plane in the air and when he tips his wing, he unknowingly grabs her heart which then zips along with him as he does rollovers and loops?

That is how I felt when Mark Peterson performed aeronautical acrobatics at last year's Wallowa County Flyin. This excitement burst in my heart again just watching a video of that event (filmed by Kyle Stangel) at the Wallowa County Pilots Association annual banquet last week.

"Do you remember the whistling?" I whispered to a friend across the table as we anticipated the presentation.

He assured me, "You can hear it on the video."

We watched so many fond memories on the screen: Cessna's of every color lined up on the grass, Miss Veedol's sassy red self parked with the other vintage aircraft, and Peterson's acrobatics in his P-51 Mustang. To see that fighter plane spin in the cerulean sky with Chief Joseph Mountain in the background took my breath away.

Flying intrigues me. Decades ago I took flying lessons-even soloed- but life interfered with my getting my pilot's license. On a trip on the Wallowa Loop Road soon after I moved here, I stopped at the Hell's Canyon Overlook and heard a roar deafening the silence.

"What IS that?" I examined the skies.

A Delta Wing Stealth Bomber appeared from the north and slowly lumbered above the Snake River, almost at eye level with me. I imagined a brontosaurus dinosaur flying..."How does it do that?"

Two summers ago I awoke to a strange sound, like a high-pitched lawn mower. But it was overhead. So I threw on some clothes and ran outside to see a powered hang-glider.

Another day an unusual sound raised my eyes upward. It was a jet being refueled in the air by another jet. The best thing about where I live is watching the private planes take off and land at Joseph Airport. "There's Andy," (the flight instructor). Or "There's Bill," or "There's Barney..."

There's a large flying community in Wallowa County that maintains backcountry strips and just has fun with airplanes. With the growing success of the Flyin, these members decided to form a nonprofit foundation that would raise funds for aviation education.

Aviation education in Wallowa County?

Yep. Classes have already begun at Joseph Charter School with expansion to Enterprise and Wallowa schools in future plans. Tobey Koehn, director of this program, has garnered funds from S. T. E. M (Science, Technology, Engineering and Math) grants and high school students currently are studying aviation and building airplane parts.

At the banquet, more exciting than the thrill of watching the DVD of last year's Flyin, was the presentation by students Ethan Pittman and his classmate, Aji, describing what they are learning. (A photo is displayed on today's blog post.) Their enthusiasm and hopes for where this curriculum can take them was infectious. The slideshow of students riveting sheet metal and of girls working on a drone brought smiles to the roomful of pilots and the rest of us who love flying.

The demand for commercial pilots, aviation mechanics, and secondary suppliers is great. To think that Wallowa County could funnel well-trained students into higher education in aeronautics, leading to well-paying jobs and satisfying career tracks is something to consider. Who knows? They may bring one of those clean industries back home.

The possibilities of where this education endeavor can take these students is as open as the vast skies above us. The Wallowa County Flyin and Pancake Breakfast, which is now a fundraiser for the North East Oregon Aviation Foundation, is scheduled for August 12. And just for fun, a fleet of 30 vintage airplanes is including a stop at Joseph Airport on July 10 on their summer schedule. Mark your calendars and watch the Chieftain for upcoming announcements. There are ways for anyone in Wallowa County to come aboard, by volunteering or purchasing sponsorships.

And while the snow has us grounded for now, I look forward to spring when pilots will push the throttle, make that motor hum and slice the air in front of Chief Joseph. Just love it!

Bill Hall approaching the Joseph Airport during the Flyin.

ARE YOU TOUGH ENOUGH?

"Katherine," a friend recently observed, "You're a pleasant person to be around, but I can see you're not someone to be trifled with."

Well, Old Man Winter has messed with me long enough. I will allow 100 words to gripe and then return to my pleasant self.

The triflings:

1. A 360 spin on top of Tollgate.

2. One week of flu.

3. Missing a turn during a white-out and becoming snowbound. I appreciated the timely arrival of Mike's Towing, but that cash layout hurt.

4. Getting high-centered in my snow and ice covered driveway four times.

5. Slipping and falling when I walked in frustration to an appointment.

6. Missing my friends because snow berms prohibited parking.

7. Being trapped in the house with a tornadic terrier and a moody shepherd dog because below zero weather kept us inside.

Okay, so that was 90 words.

In spite of all this, however, I am grateful for:

1. Heidi Muller's song, "In Wallowa." I played this several times to avoid loading up my car and leaving. (That my vehicle was stuck in the snow was irrelevant at that moment.) The refrain, "We're sticking it out in Wallowa" was quite apropos.

2.   Neighbors who helped dig me out on more than one occasion.

3.   Larry at Sports Corral placing newly purchased snow cleats on my boots. (My hands weren't strong enough.)

4.   Friends who brought me soup.

5.   People who were mindful to stay home when they had a cold so as not to share it.

6.   Lots of time to write.

7.   The local Facebook community.

8.   Dependable people from Grain Growers who kept my propane tank full.

9.   Joyful reunions with friends at Safeway when I dashed out between storms to restock.

10. Bouncing calves cavorting around their mothers along the highway between Joseph and Enterprise.

11. A sneak-away to Imnaha to see if Spring might be coming. Saw robins!

12. Reported sightings of first buttercups.

A t-shirt should be designed with these words on front "Survivor- Wallowa Winter 2017." On the back it could read "Are you tough enough?"

Speaking of tough, last week my 102 year old grandmother's sister, whom I called Aunt Carrie, passed away.

She never had children of her own, and was widowed at a young age. As a Southern lady to the nth degree, she had strong opinions (think Miss Daisy) and certain expectations of how young girls should grow up ladylike and proper. I was a consternation to her at times, but she taught me so much about determination, strength of character, and doing the right thing.

She was a classy dresser and at 100 years old sent a letter to Jergens crediting her lifelong beauty to using their lotion since she was 13 years old.

Aunt Carrie helped raise three generations of children. When she was hospitalized recently and family called, she insisted, "Don't worry about me. I'm fine."

Remembering her only brings a smile. She was tough all right, a real Steel Magnolia.

Wallowa County Chieftain, "A Wallowa Gal," February 23, 2017.

Mothers, Remember the Pickles

This time of year the world outside my window speaks of mothers. Mama cows and their calves, as black as coal, block the road ahead of me as they plod toward verdant pastures. An osprey with its beak clasping a branch wings overhead toward its nest atop a power pole. Mother sheep and goats rest in the barnyard with blades of grass protruding from either side of their mouths while lambs and kids bound about. Tails of steelhead wiggle in redds, preparing to lay eggs.

Winter and Spring play tug of war with us, snowing on daffodils, as though struggling through labor pains for new birth.

My mind drifts back to my boys (now grown men) and how much I enjoyed being their mother. Like a digital slide show, images flash before my inner eye.

Slide 356: I was trying to prop first baby Matthew, six months old, upright on the floor level waterbed. He kept tipping over to the side and I would set him up. Over to the side. Up. Again and again. He started giggling and I got tickled. It was the first deep laugh we shared.

Slide 420,761: Ten year old Sam wanted to draw on his bedroom wall. I agreed, curious about his artistic abilities. Among his sketches was an army personnel truck carrying deer, elk and moose holding rifles. Underneath was the caption, "How do you like being shot at?"

Was he going to be a pacifist? I didn't have an opinion either way, but I wondered. Today he is as big a hunter as his brother.

It seems like more pictures are of my failures, but by the grace of God, they don't remember most of them. Yet...

Slide 1,288,397: While the boys were growing up, I invited company over for dinner after church nearly every week. It was a pleasure to prepare the meal, properly decorate the table and use my fine china.

As guests complimented the display of food and dining room décor, Sam called out amidst the chatter, "Where's the pickles?"

"Pickles?"

"Pickles, Mama. You always have pickles."

Normally I included bowls of gherkin pickles and of black olives. Having overlooked pickles on my last grocery shopping, I gave no thought to the single bowl of olives now on the table.

"Sam, I didn't get pickles last time I shopped."

"But you always have pickles, Mama," he insisted.

"Sam, for this one meal there will be no pickles. But you can be assured I will not forget the pickles ever again!"

Satisfied, he quieted down and we all enjoyed a good meal.

Hours later I kissed his forehead at bedtime.

"Love you, Sam."

"I love you, too, Mama. But I can't believe you forgot the pickles."

I came across a card that indicated being a grandmother is a promotion for a job well done as a mother. Not sure I qualify. However, there are six grandchildren who know that when I arrive, there's going to be some fun!

Happy Mother's Day, especially to any MWoP's (Mothers Without Pickles). God help us all.

Wallowa County Chieftain, "A Wallowa Gal," April 28, 2017.

There's More Than Sunshine in the Spring

The sun is shining outside my patio door. Laundry is hanging on my makeshift line. These past mornings I am awakened by an introductory chorus of robin songs which crescendo into countless sparrows chirping in the lilac trees outside my bedroom window.

I've been measuring the progress of spring up the valley by the blooming of glacier lilies. In March I stopped at the Minam campground coming home from La Grande. A patch of six-inch glacier lilies with lemon yellow blooms draping over their stems greeted me.

While spending a day at Indian Crossing last week, I came upon glacier lilies just budding, and drew a deep breath of relief. Spring is here.

I am so grateful. Last winter was a tough one for many of us. For me, it was a huge learning curve. My frustration was borne from having scheduled my need to be anywhere but home for different activities. My vehicle was stuck several times in the snow. I just had to deal with it. I watched life-time residents of Wallowa County relaxing during the same winter, because they knew to stay home in such weather.

Lesson learned. I'm planning to not plan my winter by

going places. I'm grateful for my Wallowa County elders who teach me how to live and enjoy this place I call home.

I'm thankful for the people I'm acquainted with- some closer than others. While driving along the Imnaha, I encountered a fellow columnist and his friend, and had a friendly exchange about Morels, with an invitation to leave some in their truck as I made my way out.

A small celebration of my sixth decade on this earth was shared last month with friends. Nothing fancy- just the joy of getting to be with friends on a special occasion.

"What's it feel like to be 60?"

I reply, "I've heard 60 is the new 40, and I'm going to roll with that."

As Father's Day approaches, I'm grateful for the fathers who protect and provide for their children. Not all do, as evidenced in my growing up years. But I've had men at key times enter my life that filled the blank spaces. Mr. Mc-Craney, my first boss, taught this young teenager to look people directly in the eyes when talking to them. Dick Perry, another boss, recognized my potential as an engineer. He taught me how to design construction jobs and enjoyed my creativity. I call them, "My fathers by heart."

I appreciate fathers who coach baseball or softball teams and include the least player with words of encouragement. I know of ranchers who donate calves to young people for 4-H projects. There is a kind man who gave a neighborhood child a kite, just so she would look up.

So fathers, if you're out mowing the lawn or driving to Safeway, and a memory strays in that asks the question, "I wonder what ever happened to that kid?"

We're still looking up. Because of you.

Happy Father's Day.

Wallowa County Chieftain, "A Wallowa Gal," June 2, 2017.

In another part of the country, at an aviation fundraiser, pilots each drop a chicken from their planes at low altitude and the one whose chicken hits the target circle painted on the ground wins. The idea is that when the chickens flap their wings it prohibits a fatal landing, and it's funny to watch.

"That idea will never fly here," I grimaced.

My Wallowa County learning curve includes lessons on chickens. Before I arrived here, my closest association with poultry was chicken nuggets grabbed at a fast food restaurant. The basic understanding of "where do chicken nuggets come from" was there, but it didn't really matter to me. Also in the picture, a huge chicken processing plant leased hundreds of chicken farms around my former home. When the occasional Deep South heat wave killed thousands of chickens in the 300 foot long poultry houses, my only concern was to pinch my nose shut as I drove by. The smell was horrendous.

"Respect The Chicken" was not on my radar.

During my initial reconnaissance of Wallowa County, I visited the Joseph United Methodist Church. When sharing prayer requests and announcements, a woman on the front pew announced that Fred the Rooster was ready for the pot. She didn't have time to pluck it, so if anyone wanted it, let her know.

Coming from a Bible-Belt-fundamentalist-rigid-reverence background, I thought, "Wow. That's different" and decided to relocate here.

In Wallowa County, chickens are considered as pets, with given names and unique personalities.

A friend introduced me to Frozen Toes, a motherly poulter whose feet were injured with frostbite. Her coop-mate, Raspberry, was not interested in raising her chicks, so Frozen Toes took over and raised them as her own. This endeared her to me, and when I received the call one morning that a fox had raided the chicken pen and Frozen Toes was not to be found, I sobbed.

"What has become of you?" the old me asked.

Another friend has a chicken house trailer, so that when

she spends extensive time at her cabin, she can bring her chickens with her.

At a recent BBQ, several women arrived with their eggs to compare the different colors and sizes, as though speaking of their children.

While visiting another ranch woman one frigid day, she said, "Watch this."

Outside her kitchen window a hen and a young rooster were standing on a rail fence, their backs toward us.

"She's teaching him how to keep his feet warm."

It was like watching synchronized swimming at the Olympics. She slowly raised her right foot up to her feathers as snowflakes whirled about. Young Rooster did the same.

Or maybe it was chicken yoga, "Breathe in. Hold."

She eased the right foot down; he followed suit.

"Exhale."

She leaned a little to the right as she lifted her left leg. He copied. After five minutes of this back-and-forth business, I had to walk away from laughing so hard.

Perhaps owning chickens is in my future. I'll have to meditate on that.

Wildness Teaching This
Wallowa Gal

With the upcoming solar eclipse sensationalized and capitalized upon for tourism's sake, I recall a solar eclipse experience in the early 1990's.

The pending partial eclipse was mentioned in the news, but to me, it was another work day. My helper and I headed out from the office to survey. While we positioned range poles and drove stakes, the daylight began to diminish. The eclipse had begun.

We continued working, yet the shadow cast over us created a surreal feeling, as though we were working in an altered reality. Everything- the truck, our equipment, the trees in the woods, each other- all looked exactly the same, but it wasn't. It felt unnatural to be out there working, like maybe we were supposed to be somewhere else. Maybe in a church.

During lunch, my co-worker pin-holed a piece of cardboard ripped from a cracker box, then placed a second fragment underneath, and we watched the eclipse's image in silence, forgetting our sandwiches.

Wallowa County offers its own wonders. The things I've

been able to see in nature, only because I was at the right place at the right time, simply catch my breath.

A couple of months ago in the back country, I discovered an osprey nest with two fledglings. On the next visit, I was glassing these two perched on the edge of the nest, the parents gone. I nearly dropped my binoculars when the mother instantly appeared in my lens and dropped a six foot snake into the nest that was dangling lifeless from her claws. She flew away as quickly as she appeared, and the babies dropped down to eat.

I lowered the binos, "What did I just see?" Then raised them again, expecting an instant replay. Nothing.

Last hunting season, while scouting with a friend, we rounded a curve and surprised a golden eagle enjoying a road kill. So engorged with a good meal, he lifted in slow motion about 10 feet off the ground to cross to a safer spot, still within sight of his food.

"What is this place I live in?" I often ask myself.

It seems the idea of science likes to have an answer for everything. And once that was my pursuit as I graduated with an engineering degree: $1 + 1 = 2$, the area of a circle is Πr^2, a square has four equal sides.

Yet this place, the wildness of Wallowa County, cuts through my need to have answers to everything. I am more compliant with surprises, like the eclipse experience and the snake dropping. Nothing like that can be planned. When I came here, much of my life was built on pretense, that I must know everything. But this place demands that I follow its teachings rather than the other way around. And when I offer the respect that is due, I am gifted with amazing experiences that leave me in awe.

For all these and more, I am grateful.

Wallowa County Chieftain, "A Wallowa Gal," July 28, 2017.

STAYING PUT

"Man makes plans, and God laughs." This has been a recurring theme in my life. I'll be convinced a certain plan of action is exactly what I need to do, and then discover that is NOT true at all.

A couple of months ago, I notified Chieftain editor Paul Wahl that I wouldn't be writing this column anymore, and he graciously provided two more columns for my exit. Today's column would have been my last, but fortunately, I will be continuing my stories of pinnacles and pitfalls as I explore becoming a Wallowa Gal in this incredible place.

Before my readers and I continue on this adventure, I want to offer an explanation of why I thought at the time ending this column was a good idea.

I was stalked by a guy and the experience so scared me, I thought my only recourse was to move.

That's what creeps enjoy, using the power of intimidation to create fear in another and watch their reaction. From his fixation on me, my alarm created tunnel vision, thinking I had no friends here, that I didn't belong. I thought my only option was to bail out and throw away my work with the Wallowa County Museum History book, regretfully leaving behind a great committee when we are so close to sending it to the publisher. I've also been helping with a fundraiser

for a local veteran and was going to walk away from that. I was going to leave this place and people that I have grown to love and get to share stories with in this column. Even my faith went out the window, at least for a while. Terrorize and isolate. That's what creeps do.

My fear of the stalker battled with my longing to stay, and I did something I've never done before. I told my friends what was going on. One gal said, "Do you want me to straighten him out?"

This one offer gave me the courage to say, "Let me try first. You can be my backup."

I told him to leave me alone. "No," is such a powerful word when you know you mean it, even though your knees are shaking. He made a couple more creepy appearances from a distance, but I haven't seen him since.

I appreciate so much the kind comments of readers I've met on the streets...

"I'm sorry you're not going to do the column anymore."

"I really enjoy your column. It's so topical."

Words such as these gave me the courage to ask Paul if I could continue writing Wallowa Gal. He said, "Yes."

Thank you, Paul. And thank you, readers of Wallowa Gal.

Early on, in writing this column, I met a much respected Wallowa Countian in her 90's.

"I've been reading your column," she said.

I couldn't tell if she liked it or not, so I asked, "What do you think of it?"

"You'll hear about it if you get off track." (This still makes me laugh.)

So, Wallowa County, I'm staying. Until I hear otherwise.

Wallowa County Chieftain, "A Wallowa Gal," Submitted July 31, 1917.

The supportive nonprofit that keeps the county-owned Museum in Joseph operating, The Friends of the Wallowa County Museum, has been soliciting family stories since 2014 to be published as a history book. Several of the members were involved in the publication of a 1983 history book that is now out of print and considered an heirloom.

Earlier this year, I agreed to help them move their gathered stories into publication, and what fun and how interesting that is. The History Book Committee members are hardworking and it seems they love Wallowa County stories as well as their own children. Though we don't have a specific date for the books on hand, we're aiming for the end of the year. Watch for notices of pre-sale ordering.

We lost a couple of figures of living history in recent weeks. Bill Bailey of Imnaha lived to 101 years old and Arnold Schaeffer was a heartstone of Lower Valley. Though I never was acquainted with Bill, I can only imagine what stories he held of Wallowa County.

In February 2014, having lived here for only two weeks, I was assigned to write a magazine article about mules. After the guidelines were offered, I called Janie Tippett, "I don't know a thing about mules!" She gave me names of five outfitters to contact for interviews, and Arnold entered my life.

He must have read "sucker for stories" on my forehead, for the interview lasted longer than I planned. I left saying, "You have too much to tell for one article. Your stories need to be in a book. I'll be back."

Thus a three year friendship was borne. The first book of what was later dubbed "The High Mountain Series" was "Mack the Mule," a fascinating story of the Schaeffer family guiding from Lapover Pack Station with Mack.

Within a few weeks after the Mack book, Arnold called. "I've got some more stories."

"I'll be down tomorrow." From that came "A Ride to the Promise Land."

His phone calls became like bait cast in my direction. Numerous trips to his home produced more books, "Mama Wapiti," "Doc Adair," and "Crow Cabin."

In the mix were my taking him for rides. At Two Pan, hunters unloading their stock gathered round Arnold for some good visiting. Headed back home, I said, "You're a rock star, Arnold."

He grinned, "Isn't that a kick?"

We had a wonderful visit when I learned he was in the hospital a couple of months ago. Yet I wondered when I left how much longer he would last. Soon after, Mary at The Bookloft called several times wanting more of Arnold's books. When making the delivery, I asked her, "What's going on? I thought things were winding down with these books."

She replied, "Arnold's in the hospital selling his books."

"That Arnold!" I still laugh about that.

My appreciation goes out to his family who shared Arnold with me and heartfelt condolences to all who knew him. We certainly lost a treasure.

Wallowa County Chieftain, "A Wallowa Gal," Submitted Sept. 29, 2017.

SHE HAD HIS SIX

In spite of my efforts to become a Wallowa Gal, my Southern roots make occasional appearances.

A fundraiser was held during the summer to build a shed for Vietnam Marine Joe Lewellyn in Joseph. Money was raised, the shed is completed and it now shelters his new Action Track Chair. Joe is tickled happy.

We are now putting together a Chili Feed for Veterans on Saturday, November 11. Chow will be served at 11:30 a.m. at The Place (next to Joseph United Methodist Church), 303 S. Lake Street. With seating limited to 100 people, we are selling tickets for $10 each for sponsors and friends of veterans to purchase and then give to their favorite veterans. These funds will help pay for the event and future activities for local veterans.

Free tickets are available for veterans and their families, veterans' widows and parents at Community Bank branches in Wallowa, Enterprise and Joseph. Tickets may be purchased at The Bookloft in Enterprise. Other locations may be posted on Facebook.

The Southern roots thing comes in because we're serving Texas chili, which means, NO BEANS. I didn't realize this could be an issue until after the Wallowa County Stockgrowers Association agreed to donate the ground beef. Oh, well. Still learning. So if veterans are brave enough to try something different...Y'all come!

Arion Canniff (co-owner with wife Amy Wolf of the new Dog Spot going in at the former Silver Lake Bistro location) is cooking. Homemade Jam is playing. And friends are stepping up to serve. We're looking forward to a community-wide expression of "Welcome Home" to our veterans.

This poem is posted on my blog. Feel free to share it as a gift to your favorite veteran for Veterans Day:

She Had His Six

"She's yours, not mine"
He was gruff to say
Of the pup squirming in my arms
But she won him over
With soft brown eyes
Her honesty was her charm

A cellophane pop
The grab of his cap
It was time to have a smoke
She stood at the door
To the sacred porch
Then she gave his leg a poke
How often I gazed
Through the curtained glass
At the two who were now a pair
Not a word was said
Not a move was made
But I saw the thousand yard stare
Without a sound
He told her of
The Hueys that swarmed like bees
The tracers of light
The ear-numbing booms
The blood, the cries and the screams
"We didn't have friends.
Just 'Buddy' would do"

He told his little girl
She wiggled her tail
And nudged his hand
His fingers would then unfurl
By then I ran
To the kitchen sink
Pretending I didn't know
She was on his six
In the places where
His wife was forbidden to go
And now he lies
On a hospice bed
Agent Orange counts the rise of his chest
She nuzzles his hand
On top of her head
Too soon is his final breath
She had his six
Like no one did
He was safe with her along
His little girl dog
Her mission complete
She trailed him all the way home.

Wallowa County Chieftain, "A Wallowa Gal," For Nov. 1, 2017.

The Wallowa County Museum's history book, "Wallowa County- A Continuation," is available for pre-sale. Though we're nearing the end of final editing, and the publisher will have it back to us by first quarter of 2018, we thought it would make a great gift idea. That is, when you purchase it as a gift, you will receive a decorative gift notification to hand to your loved one.

The stories are fascinating to me. Many of those who settled this place served in the Civil War. Perhaps those veterans found the isolation and beauty of this landscape a place of peace, a place to get on with their lives as best they could. The family histories reveal spouses who pulled together like a matched pair, carving a life and a family out of this hard land, getting each day's work done. There are the children who died and the marriages that didn't last. In family photos, I examine the women's faces- as honest, as worn, and as beautiful as the canyons of lower Imnaha.

In reading and formatting these stories for printing, I see the difficulties that plowed the hearts of these people left crevasses filled with passion. When they sang and danced and loved, they shared the joy of making it another season. They helped neighbors who had been burned out or couldn't plant because of a farm accident, for on any given day, they could be next.

"Who owns the land?" is often debated. To me, the better question is, "Who gets to manage it?" Anyone who has been through a natural disaster, such as an earthquake or a wildfire or tornado, knows the utter powerlessness in the face of earth's forces. Scientists and academics strive to define and explain every minutiae of the earth's activities, positing that greater knowledge grants greater privilege of ownership. Yet the seasons which bring moisture, or not, the winds that let trees stand, or not, the mountains which hold snow, or not- the earth is going to allow what it will tolerate, until it doesn't.

Lifelong Wallowa Countians who made a life here learned

to cooperate with what the land provided. As many who succeeded, there were that many who left.

Beneath the materialism of this month, another story is heralded, told in a book that has been the #1 best-seller since its initial printing. "Basic Instructions Before Leaving Earth" leads the reader on a wild tale describing an unseen power. He creates teachable moments and love-filled solutions for people whose backs are against the wall, who don't know which way to turn, who rail at God then are answered with quiet whispers of hope. If a person is looking for a Joseph Campbell narrative arc, stay away from this book. If a reader anticipates a John-Wayne-kind-of-character, "Shoot 'em all. Ask questions later," this story won't make sense. If logic is sought, forget about it.

But, if you like mystery and romance and adventure and murder and betrayal and redemption and can consider that love made itself known in the birth of an unlikely baby, read

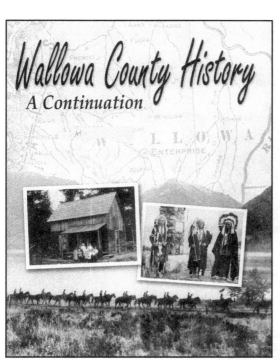

The Book. Study the lyrics of Christmas hymns or visit a Christmas Eve service. Afterward, go to Wallowa Lake and listen to "O Holy Night" on your player as you gaze upon the stars illuminating Chief Joseph Mountain. For those with eyes to see and ears to hear, it's a wonderful story with a happy ending.

Merry Christmas to all.

Wallowa County Chieftain, "A Wallowa Gal," Submitted Dec. 1, 2017.

If I were to calculate the cost of my lost time looking for misplaced items, the amount would near one million dollars. I'm sure of it.

In early September, I misplaced my cell phone. Perhaps it's an internal message to "Slow down" or "pay attention" but my angst in looking for it makes my concentration worse, not better.

Based on my history of finding lost items, I searched in my shoes, in the refrigerator, and scoured my car. I suspected my pup Petey, but he took the fifth. I even raised the bed linens, careful not to disturb Mosie the cat, but did not see it.

My friends generously offered suggestions, most of which I had already examined. Nada. At 30 days I surrendered and shopped for a new cell phone.

"I'd like one just like the one I lost."

The roll of the representative's eyes communicated her disdain while, with great effort of politeness, she explained

how outdated my old one was. This concerned me because that first smart phone was a great technological improvement from the flip phone I had used for years.

Side story: I lost that flip phone while hiking along Upper Imnaha. Ten months later, a representative texted me on my new (at the time) phone asking if I had lost a cell phone.

"Yes."

"I have it here in Pasco."

"How'd you get it?"

"A lady found it last summer while hiking and just turned it in."

And that was it. No effort to return it to me. No further explanation... I am left baffled at these odd things that happen.

So, this past October I purchased another smart phone. (Smart phone is a misnomer, for they leave me feeling anything but.) The next day while changing the sheets (I had to make Mosie move), there was the missing phone. She had been resting on it all the time. My friends who know Mosie agreed that was just like her to do that- watch me fret over such a thing and not say a word to help. So cat!

My new phone anticipates what I'm going to say and literally inserts words into my communication that are not intended.

I was texting a mutual friend that I would not be attending a pot luck at Vickey's. Just as I hit SEND, I noticed, "Can't make it to Bucket's." Immediately I sent a second text with correction trying to explain what the phone was doing. "Phone toes for me." Another quick fix, "Talks not toes."

In preparing for the Veterans Day chili feed, I was texting a friend about sponsors who donated food and saw the phone interjected "Good" donations. Exasperated, I sent off the correction, "Food not good."

"Why are you telling me the food is not good?" she responded.

This led to an audio phone call to clarify, which was difficult because I was laughing so hard.

Right now, two tin cans with a string connecting them looks quite appealing.

Wallowa County Chieftain, "A Wallowa Gal," Submitted Dec. 27, 2017.

This milder winter is certainly a blessing and a relief. More of my distress during last year's winter was due to not being prepared with proper supplies and adequate food. All is going well now- haven't had any real emergencies other than at this moment I'm staying with a friend because I have no heat in the house. Grain Growers will replace my propane stove soon.

Last summer, while bagging Imnaha country blackberries to freeze, I wondered if they would grow here in the valley. About four berries were placed in a glass dish next to the sink to let dry. I'd plant them soon.

As weeks passed I became worried about my eyesight. My eyes felt tired and weak from long hours on my laptop as I worked on the history book. I scheduled an eye appointment with an ophthalmologist. In 2014 he had diagnosed a condition that would cause me to be blind in three years. Yet in 2015 that condition had left by following his vitamin regimen. That dilemma raised its head though. Is that why I was having trouble with my vision?

Cooler nights signaled snow was coming soon. As I puttered around the house I'd hear a bump in the kitchen that I assumed was Petey Pup and ignored it. My little garden plot in the back yard was already dug. There was no sensibility

in planting the seeds at this time of year... it was more about holding on to my last chance to stick something in the ground.

I noticed tiny segments of the blackberries in the space behind my kitchen faucet and the wall. "How did those get there?" I questioned. But I scooped them up, grabbed the dish holding the others and headed out the door.

"There now," I spoke, patting the dirt over the seeds. "Let's see how this turns out."

Within a few days, I found evidence that more were living with me than just Petey. Mice droppings were scattered in the cabinets and drawers under the sink. I stared blankly at the wall, then burst out laughing.

"Oh, smart, Katherine. I think you planted mouse turds in your garden!"

I explained my diminishing vision (but not the turd planting) to the eye doctor.

"Your tests look good. In fact, your vision has improved," he looked at me. "Let me see your glasses."

He held them up to the light. "Do you ever clean these?"

Pause. "Whenever I think of it."

"How often is that?"

"Maybe once a week." I felt two inches tall.

"How about three times a day?" he instructed.

Laying my head on the car door before unlocking it, I bemoaned, "It's so hard being me!"

So now I cast a wary eye toward that bare patch of dirt by my fence.

Warming days coming and after the robins return, I will have to face the inevitable and examine last year's plantings.

If tiny noses with whiskers appear, and beady black eyes return my gaze, you'll be the first to know.

Wallowa County Chieftain, "A Wallowa Gal," Submitted Feb. 2, 2017.

LIVING WITH CANCER

Outside my window a big dump of snow is falling from the upper heights. I am thankful for a warm house- thank you Grain Growers (Adam, Caleb and Aaron.)

Having recently learned that a close friend of mine was diagnosed with cancer, I stopped by to offer him a word of encouragement. He and his wife have quite the journey ahead of them.

My husband Richard and I walked a similar path nine years ago. From the beginning, Richard's prognosis was terminal. His chemotherapy was to slow the tumor's growth and buy him time. "Buy him time for what?" I bitterly wondered. I was afraid hopelessness would kill him before the cancer.

We lived like the steel ball in a pinball machine. We never knew, day by day, what would flip our course of action. The big Cs were the Cancer, then Chemo, and finally, we settled into Change. Constant change.

A game changer for us was when I told him, "From this day on, you are living with cancer, not dying from it. We are going to find something to be thankful for."

In appreciation for the nurses at the cancer center, he gave them one of his paintings. This was a huge boost to him. When radiation treatment began, he asked me to draw a happy face on his chest with a marker. The radiology tech burst out laughing when he raised his shirt. She called in the team and giggles regaled that hour.

Our monthly cycle was his infusion, then intense sickness for three weeks with occasional moments of relaxation. By the fourth week he would feel well enough to do something, so we'd go out to eat, or go fishing, or go to a movie.

In March 2009 the cancer had spread to his brain. One day I came home and found him with my Bible. "I think there's something in here I should know," he said. I was too emotional to explain things, so a friend came over and shared the story of Jesus.

"That's so simple," Richard stated, and that afternoon he was baptized for the forgiveness of sins.

What astounds me still is the peace it brought him. All was forgiven- what happened in Vietnam (I was told only a fragment of it all), and the storm of his alcoholic years (he was sober 37 years when he passed) and the wreckage of his marriages (I was his fourth wife)... it was all gone. He no longer cussed (this was huge, for he was a sailor after all.) I don't know if he let all that go, or if he was released from it. It wasn't about church, for he didn't go. He simply lived in peace until his last breath.

I reminded my friend the other day that this was another bend on his journey, that each day, he was living with cancer and not dying.

And on the way home, I finally realized what Richard and I were buying time for.

Wallowa County Chieftain, "A Wallowa Gal," Submitted Mar. 2, 2018.

109

A Vote That Values
Our Community

My philosophy is to add value to each person, each place I encounter. I seem to fail as much as succeed, but the striving for such leads to a better day. I've been thinking about what adds value to community.

Incrementally, Wallowa County residents are facing decisions on self-sustainability. The County removed funding for the WC Museum in Joseph. Museum Board members will soon publish "Wallowa County History- A Continuation," sales of which will support operation of the Museum. What is the value of the Museum? The collection of memorabilia and stories retains our community's identity, a vital component of the culture we love so well.

The County has reduced funds to imprison criminals. Violators are processed through the court in a quasi "catch and release" system. Criminals such as drug dealers and "tweakers" (meth addicts) are free to ride bicycles along the streets through all hours of the night. So now we lock our doors. What is the value of public safety? How important is trusting that our personal safety, as well as our belongings, are protected? Do we form secret vigilantes and designate a "hanging judge?" I have no answers.

Funding for the Wallowa County Library has been removed, which brings us to an upcoming vote to establish a Library District. The convenience of Kindle and downloadable books can appear to make libraries obsolete. What is the value of libraries these days? I can vouch personally on that...

Growing up with alcoholic parents, I was silenced as a little girl- not allowed to believe the horrors I witnessed, not allowed to admit the screaming and crying I heard, not allowed to speak of my fears. The library was my safe place. As I pulled open the heavy oak door, the smell of old books welcomed me. The white haired librarian with horn-rimmed glasses became a mother-figure, nurturing me with books.

"I think you'll like this one," she smiled one day, handing me a biography of Helen Keller. I identified with the girl, imprisoned without the ability to communicate who she was. When her teacher finally connected with Helen through sign language, I cried with tears of understanding and hope. Hope that one day, I might connect with others through my words.

My husband Richard convinced me that I was a good writer. And the responses of you, my readers- cards, emails, comments of appreciation you've made when I've met you on the street- have added value to my writing.

I had a bad fall on March 5 and am currently silenced by a serious concussion/ traumatic brain injury. Doc says no reading, no writing, no computer screen for several months- maybe a year. (A friend is typing this for me.) Again, I turn to the library. I contacted Susan at the Wallowa County Library and now listen to audiobooks- connecting me to words, connecting me to stories, connecting me to writers.

Readers need writers. It's a relationship that goes beyond the binding of a book, the ink on the page. It's an exchange of ideas, an agreement or disagreement on the plausible or unbelievable. The words of writers give readers ideas and phrases needed to express themselves.

And writers need readers. In the telling and the listening, we give each other voice. You have given me all that and more by following this column. I began this column to share the fun, foibles and a few tears in my attempt to learn this place. Last week, a friend introduced me to someone, "This is Katherine Stickroth. She's a real Wallowa gal!" My heart smiled.

That I may focus on my recovery, this is the closing of

the Wallowa Gal column. Yet I'll still be around. God bless each one of you for honoring me with your readership.

I ask you to support the Library District with your vote. I'm confident the Library District ballot issue will pass because that's what we do- the right thing for each other, in our Wallowa County.

Wallowa County Chieftain, "A Wallowa Gal," Submitted Mar. 28, 2018.

CATCHING UP WITH A WALLOWA GAL

My eyes locked on the mountains as I rounded the curve approaching Enterprise from La Grande.

"Home."

It's been a hard year. In April 2018, I wrote my last column, informing y'all of my brain injury suffered from a hard smack on the head the previous month. My damaged vision prohibited any time on my laptop. I could not filter what came out of my mouth, with errant thoughts and then words flailing about like an out of control water hose at full force. Severe headaches and burning eyes left me unable to take care of myself.

In June 2018, another blow to my head from falling landed me in the ER. They said once you have a concussion, it's likely you'll fall more often.

Nurse practitioner Billie Suto and physical therapist Jerry Ivy were among my many Wallowa County angels. I cannot name the numerous members of the community who gave me rides to appointments when I couldn't drive and fixed meals when I couldn't cook. I thank them all.

Neurologist Dr. Quinto in La Grande recommended treatment at Grande Ronde Hospital's concussion rehab program. Unwilling to travel twice a week through the Minam during the winter, I arranged to stay in La Grande to focus on getting well. What a hard winter it was there, and even worse, I heard, over here.

From my friend's house, I would gaze across Grande Ronde Valley to the western side of the Wallowas. Veterans and other friends from the County called to check on me. I longed to be home and well.

The concussion rehab treatment launched me forward into recovery. I'm not cured, but I am improving every day and know how to treat any symptoms that come up.

I am so grateful to be home now. Better able to think, to get around, and now, to write. Five years ago, I landed in the County a stranger not knowing a soul. The welcome I received then and especially your kindness from the past year have disarmed me. The brain injuries, which I thought were the worst thing to happen to me, have turned out to be the best thing ever. Those blows to my head knocked out the stubborn, self-reliant pride that said I could make it through life on my own.

I give thanks and praise to the Jesus who can change a person's heart by showing the goodness of others. When I sit at the lake and meditate with Chief Joseph Mountain before me, I think of the powerful force that pushed the molten rock to such great height. It represents to me the immensity of His love, so great and all-encompassing, that led me to Wallowa County and holds me here, still.

If you see me around, be sure to say hello. You may have to re-introduce yourself, for I'm having to relearn everything and everybody. But this I will never forget, how very, very grateful I am to call Wallowa County "Home," because of you.

Wallowa County Chieftain, "A Wallowa Gal," Published April 2019.

CLOSING - FIRST BUTTERCUP

It is pre-dawn, and the kindling in the woodstove is popping. Petey is still sleeping. Morning's light slowly reveals misting rain dropping into the Minam Canyon where my cabin is nestled on a slope.

The silence is hushed with only the Wallowa River rushing below me. The forest trees still surround me. The canyon walls continue to tower above me.

I wish it would stay like this forever.

But at this time, the world, our nation, our state and Wallowa County is under siege to the coronavirus. Individuals are practicing "social distancing" to avoid spreading the contagion. In the sequestering, we are limited in employment, shopping, transportation, schooling, and communication.

In my writing of this, I searched my thesaurus for synonyms of the word "change." I found "adjustment, development, modification, transformation..." All these words describe how we must respond to this natural disaster. Wallowa Countians are good at this.

I will be temporarily leaving The County tomorrow to "Stay Safe and Stay Alive" at the home of other friends as the national response trickles down into my life. My packing has intersected with efforts to finalize the submittal of the contents of this book to Linda Bauck who is designing its layout.

My sorrow over leaving has been couched in laughter as Linda and I have reviewed the stories. In searching for just the right photo to match each story, I am reminded of my six years here with great joy.

I moved here as a confused and lonely woman. Family disturbances, the loss of my husband, an "empty-nest," ...

what was I to do with my life? And who am I, anyway? This was the first time, ever, I had been on my own.

Wallowa County. Your landscape has been a balm for my troubled soul. Your mountain peaks have stood firm as something I could count on. Your valley vistas have opened my heart. Your canyon walls have embraced me. Your running waters have soothed me. Your great lake has brought me peace. The songs of the prairie birds have taught me to sing again.

Your people have disarmed me. The ebb and flow of county-wide relationships have mended my heart as worn-out socks are darned. The dark threads only make the light colored fibers shine brighter. I am laughing again, more at myself than anyone else. In the recounting of my fun and foibles here, I have found it is okay to not take myself so seriously.

That's a good thing.

Wallowa County. You have given me stories, too many to be bound in this one book. I am a writer, and stories are like manna from heaven. I feed on them and share them with others. More of my writing is found on awallowagal.com.

This writing life of mine has now shifted to stories of a wild, yellow fuzzy dog thing I call Petey Podengo. My worldview is now through the tall pointed ears of this little guy who drives me crazy, yet I cannot live without him. My dog has a blog. You can follow us on his website peteypodengo.com.

The things he and I get into...well, it isn't always pretty, but it sure is fun.

Because the canyons are at a lower elevation, the warmer days of spring come earlier than "on top." Bright yellow buttercups are a welcome assurance that better days are coming. Among the canyon-dwellers, when a person finds his or her first buttercup, it is picked and given to a dear friend as a token of how meaningful their relationship is.

Consider this book my "first buttercup" to you. Wherever I go, Wallowa County is stamped on my heart. Thank you for that.

Hope you enjoyed the ride! I sure did.

God bless you, everyone.

A Wallowa Gal,

Katherine Stickroth

March 29, 2020

Richard

ABOUT THE AUTHOR

Encouraged by her husband, Richard, that she was indeed a writer, Katherine Stickroth's conversational style and gentle wit invite the reader to spend time with her. A natural storyteller, her articles have been published in newspapers and magazines across the United States. The addition of Petey, a spunky Portugese Podengo terrier, completes her family of two grown sons, their wonderful wives and her seven grandchildren. Whether in the back country wilderness or in her garden, Stickroth enjoys gathering stories in the Pacific Northwest where she resides.

9 781087 926902